Mastering Diversity

"We go together or not at all!"

Bernie Davies

All rights reserved. No part of this book may be used, replicated, or reproduced in any manner whatsoever without the written permission of the author except in the case of quotations of not more than 25 words and which are solely for the purpose of critical articles or reviews. Although the author and publisher have made every effort to ensure that the information in this book is correct at the time of going to print, the author and publisher do not assume and therefore disclaim liability to any party. The author and the publisher will not be held responsible for any loss or damage same for that caused by their negligence. Although the author and the publisher have made every reasonable attempt to achieve accuracy in the content of this book, they assume no responsibility for errors or omissions. You should only use this information as you see fit. Any use is at your own risk. You must act responsibly and sensibly in your use of the information and your life and circumstances may not be suited to the examples shared within these pages. How you choose to include this information in this book within your own life is completely your own responsibility and at your own risk.

Copyright © 2023 Bernie Davies

All rights reserved.

ISBN: 978-1-914439-11-7

"Bernie, a Lawyer, TEDx Speaker, Author, Diversity & Entrepreneurship Leader, Mentor, Coach and Publisher, Multi-awardee, has an indomitable spirit across the field of Business Management, Leadership and Self Development. Her warmth, capability skills and ability to make people feel valued contributed to her success towards a business owner and author.

She is an exemplary role model for other ethnic minority Welsh women and is inherent in uniting people from diverse communities, championing the needs of the disadvantaged. She was recently celebrated for her lifetime achievements by the Ethnic Minority Welsh Women Achievement Association (EMWWAA)."

PROFESSOR MEENA UPADHYAYA OBE PHD, FRCPATH, FLSW

DEDICATION

I would like to dedicate this book to all the little girls who once feared they would never be heard. All the little girls who suffered shame, rejection, bullying, insecurities and felt they just did not quite fit in. All the young women who have suffered violence, domestic abuse, discrimination, been misunderstood and not quite being able to speak up.

I want to dedicate this book to the young boys who struggle to find their place, to know who they are and to figure out what being a REAL man is all about, because they did not have a daddy who showed them that. I would like to dedicate this book to all the disabled, to all the nerds, and all the people that are displaced in one way or another. Displaced geographically, displaced by ideals, displaced by religious affiliation, displaced by sexual orientation, displaced by limiting capabilities, displaced by not thinking feeling acting and being what the world calls normal.

I would just like to dedicate this book the incredible potpourri of people, Nations, cultures, Creed, cognitions, and ways of being that is the fabric of which the Welsh landscape is comprised. Why do I want to focus on Wales? Wales is now my home and has been my home since 2006. But most importantly it is the place I became acutely aware of the importance of deliberate diversity. It is also the place that I came face to face with unconscious bias, discrimination, and racism. And it is also the place where I found true acceptance, and also the place that I found "no closed doors" for a very long time. Wales is the place, I realised that being different was actually an advantage.

You might ask, "What are you saying Bernie? You are contradicting yourself?" It may sound like a contradiction, but this is my truth and my experience is not unique. Moreover, it highlights that in a world where you can find hate separation discrimination and bias...in that same world you can find acceptance, unconditional love, and togetherness.

This is why I am writing this book about mastering diversity. And even more so why I will be focusing most of my anecdotal research evidence on Wales. Wales is now my home and there is a saying that *charity begins at home*. So my focus is not to heal the world. My focus is to heal my world. My beautiful, green, lush world…Wales. And to bloom where I am planted.

Table of Contents

DEDICATION iv

ACKNOWLEDGMENTS vii

1 WHAT'S ALL THIS FUSS ABOUT DIVERSITY AND INCLUSION? 11

2 INFORMATION BUBBLES & ECHO CHAMBERS 25

3 GROUPTHINK 34

4 Cognitive Diversity 45

5 ALLYSHIP 54

6 PRIVILEGE 65

7. BRIDGING THE GAP- Use Your Power 80

8 REPRESENTATION-Being Seen and heard 87

9 HIDING IN PLAIN SIGHT - The Hidden Diversity 104

10 MASTERING DIVERSITY 115

CONCLUSION 122

ABOUT THE AUTHOR 123

ACKNOWLEDGMENTS

I would like to honor and note the value of certain key people in my life and work over the last 23 years. The reason I have singled out 23 years out of a 60 year lifespan, is simply to focus on one aspect of my development in these 60 years. That is, the development of an understanding of **who I am**, in terms of my differences, in terms of what it means within the space that I live and work, in terms of what it means, in respect to how I value others, how I engage with others, and how I come to understand the needs of others and not just of myself.

I learned a lot moving to the United Kingdom and experiencing several culture shocks. I want to thank the people that embraced me. Vashti Lee and your beautiful family. You know how much you saved my life back then. I thank Bradford council, who when I launched a charity in 2001, when I was struggling myself with joblessness, and I launched that charity to support refugees and asylum seekers and Brits who were struggling with the social welfare system, Bradford council got behind me. When I had an opportunity to take my message to the United Nations, in Switzerland Geneva, they paid for me to go and for my daughter to go and for someone else to go and look after her while I spoke at such and elevated platform

I would like to thank Walker Morris solicitors in Leeds and DLA Direct solicitors in Bradford who gave me the opportunity to launch into my legal career after four years in the wilderness so to speak. Thank you for giving me an opportunity to add value, introduce new concepts, new training, new ways of dealing with staff, and new ways of leading... I thank you.

I would also like to acknowledge Helen Molyneux past Head of Newlaw solicitors, who gave me an opportunity to head their property department in Cardiff Bay, Wales. This despite the fact that I was suffering from serious female problems which were going to take a while to be dealt with as an operation was required. Despite knowing that, she still offered me the job and gave me a platform in Wales that has been the best opportunity I have had for my career and for my purpose since coming to the United Kingdom.

I would like to thank the very many organisations including the Welsh Government, Cardiff Council Economic Development Team, the banks including NatWest, British business bank, Barclays, HSBC which have given me a platform and an opportunity to share my expertise in entrepreneurship and diversity and inclusion.

I want to thank all the universities- University of South Wales, Cardiff University, Cardiff Metropolitan University Center for Entrepreneurship, Swansea University Bay and Singleton campus, University of Wales Trinity St David, and Bangor University who have given me an opportunity to contribute to their entrepreneurship and diversity and inclusion programs.

I would like to thank Ethnic Minority Welsh Women Achievers Association for their Lifetime Achievement Award for my DEI work! I would also like to thank Black History Wales for their Excellence in Business Award and a seat on their Management Committee, Race Council Cymru, African Community Centre Wales for their Swansea Black Icon Award, Public Services Ombudsman for Wales for making me the first Black woman appointed to their Advisory Panel, FIO Arts Charity (serving Global Majority Artists) for appointing me a Trustee and Women's Business Club for their Diversity and Inclusion and Speaker of the Year awards, Chwarae Teg, Welsh ICE and so many more. This list is not exhaustive. There are so many more that I could name…not to mention individuals… Suffice it to say, that I would not have had the richness of experience and firsthand knowledge and information to be able to share with you in this book, if I had not had the privilege of working and supporting these fantastic organisations and learning from the most incredibly diverse mix of amazing colleagues, one could ask for.

I am most grateful for my wonderful bi-racial, eclectic blended family consisting of my 4 amazing children, Jerome, Joel, Matthew, and Barri-Allison. My 2 stepchildren, Matthew and Rebecca, my Godson Samuel and our 12 beautiful grandchildren. My wonderful wind beneath my wings…husband Mark! There are no words! It has been a painful and joyful journey mixing families, cultures, beliefs, and expectations. I have enjoyed everything there has been to enjoy and I am looking forward to growing to a very old age with them. Thank you!

WHAT'S ALL THIS FUSS ABOUT DIVERSITY AND INCLUSION?

1 WHAT'S ALL THIS FUSS ABOUT DIVERSITY AND INCLUSION?

An idea that is of its time and in its time, is inevitably at risk of falling prey to suspicion, fear and facing hostile resistance. It is not enough to recognise the importance and imperative of any ideal if we are not prepared to sustain our efforts to be a part of its coming to term and finding its rightful place.

Whilst Diversity, Equity, and Inclusion, has been par for the course for me…it is anathema to some…but who am I to judge?

I grew up in a remarkably diverse context with my teachers showing up in Saris, African dress, and others, white…of American, German, Spanish and Jewish heritage, to name a few. My classmates were just as, if not more diverse. But that was my lived experience.

I recently shared this story before a multi-national organisation with upper management, Industry leaders and decision makers at an extremely prominent level, in attendance. Whilst there was an overwhelmingly positive response to my Talk on Allyship, there was the criticism that I did not refer to the intolerance that exists within Caribbean cultures for the LGBTQ community. In my defense, I was talking about MY own lived experience as a child and young lady. At that time, it was colour / race / culture centric. Yes, I was from a deeply religious family, but the religious demographic did not play a part in my socialisation, apart from the fact that going to Church was a major part of my upbringing.

I did not personally know anyone that suffered from a physical disability (except my brother's best friend and he did not seem to suffer because of it) and so that did not form part of my early years' contemplation or retrospection. My story was therefore limited to colour and culture and I inadvertently made some of my audience feel othered. To make matters worse, a part of my presentation was a reference to the great Chimamanda Ngozi Adiche's Ted Talk, "The Danger of the Single Story." It is my belief that the stories we tell form the narrative we weave, the influence we wield, the minds we master and the selves we replicate.

Therefore, if we remain contained within the walls of our own lived experiences, to the exclusion of an understanding of that of others, we run the risk of falling short of the mark and making peace with mediocrity and fools of ourselves.

I am not making any claim to being an expert nor am I declaring that I have all the answers. I am simply making my statements based on my experiences and those of others I have had the privilege to live amongst and work with, in the pursuit of a more diverse and fair way of being.

So why am I writing this book? The main reason is to make the point that to master diversity, one has to understand it in its many facets, intersections, and contradictions. Does one even truly contemplate the distinction between **Diversity, Equity, Equality, Inclusion** and **Belonging (DEI)**? I will develop on this, later on in this book.

Diversity and My Work

Over the years I have supported the Welsh government, major banks, and universities' entrepreneurship programmes. I have trained large and small corporate teams and mentored entrepreneurs. My insider information is that there is a head knowledge of the importance of diverse teams BUT a failure…for the most part…to truly come to terms with what that should look like.

I have been a part of projects or and continue to support projects, which have as their goal, supporting those from Black Asian and Minority Ethnic groups (BAME groups), females, under twenty-fives and those with the other protected diversity characteristics. I have observed at times that there has been a distinct lack of Allyship, tolerance and fair play being applied in running some of these initiatives. I have observed unconscious bias, groupthink, and excluding behaviours at the hands of those with the stated intent of being the change. I can also wholeheartedly say that the majority of those whom I have witnessed, who have perpetuated these negative behaviours, do genuinely want to make a difference. So the question therefore is… "if so, why so?"

In my experience, most businesses have a DEI Policy. Most employees have no real idea what their company's DEI Policy is! Some workplaces tick the box with a training session and some even go as far as having an expert in to assess their systems and give them the golden seal of tokenistic approval.

But how much of this is actually followed through and translates into a positive experience for those marginalised groups within these businesses? How many influencers and people in positions of authority make it their duty to encourage and mandate equality, inclusion, and practice allyship in the workplace?

My view is the difficulty with achieving a fair, welcoming, and safe society for ALL (which is what all this fuss is really about) is in changing hearts, minds, mindsets, and deep-seated beliefs. We will always be on the "back foot" if we do not reach hearts and minds and thereby change behaviours and attitudes.

For example, some of us do not even know why we are angry! Why am I happy to be told off by a white, middle aged dark suited man for something I am not convinced I got wrong on the job BUT jump up and down in uncontrollable rage if a Black, female, younger boss asks ME to do something differently, because that is the way she likes it? God forbid, if she also comes from the Welsh Valleys and I am from Cardiff, Wales.

Let us not even go there with "gingers" / "redheads" as opposed to blondes and the "holy" divide between football regions. The societal hierarchies are alive and well and we are very keen to remind people of whom they are and "where to," they need to return…and I mean in the same country and sometimes only a few miles apart.

So my reason for writing this book is to open up more conversations around mindsets and how they affect a diverse and unequal society and workplace. My view is there is money to be made by truly embracing diversity and inclusion. Truly embracing diversity requires an **equitable= fair approach. Equality and Equity are not the same.** Two people can be equals but they can still be meted out with a separate set of circumstances or treatment. In order to reduce your frown lines, let me explain. In a particular legal practice, there are legal clerks, law associates, partners et ux. All their legal clerks have an equal position, but not all might be given the same opportunity for upward mobility. Meaning they are not treated equitably. The same goes for the lawyer who remains an Associate until retirement (or moving elsewhere for escalation) in comparison to their counterpart who made Partner after 2 years! Are we getting it now?

The challenge, therefore, is not only to recruit diverse talents, origins, and expertise! It is recruiting the talent, skill and experience we are looking for, that does NOT share how we view the world, or our religion, sexual orientation, body size, race, and gender. It is also going that step further, from simply **including** them in our books, but to also deliberately making consistent moves to giving them a sense of **BELONGING**. That unfortunately, becomes a step too far…for some.

There is no question that, the companies that are thriving and boast a wholesome and productive work culture, are the ones that undertake deliberately diverse recruitment and practice allyship within the workplace. Their team leaders are aware of privilege and their responsibility to influence attitudes. They are intentional in monitoring and rewarding inclusive behaviours, which lead to a sense of belonging. They are deliberate in ensuring that no one feels undervalued in meetings and all opinions are treated with the same respect. Micro-aggressions are identified AND if not eradicated...they are appropriately managed.

DIVERSITY AND ENTREPRENEURSHIP

It is unequivocal, that diversity in Entrepreneurship is extremely vital! Innovative products and disruptive thinking are the life blood of industry. Gender has always been a topic when diversity and inclusion is being discussed, as women are still outnumbered as entrepreneurs and female Founders are not preferred by investors.

In March 2019, the UK Treasury commissioned NatWest's then CEO, Alison Rose, to lead an independent review of female entrepreneurship. The report interestingly asserted, that if women started and scaled new businesses at the same rate as men, up to £250bn of new value could be added to the UK economy. The 2022 report update was promising as it stated, that "more than 140,000 companies were established by all-women teams" in 2021 and the figure was set to grow by a third each year.

Interestingly, the Federation of Small Businesses on their website (https://www.fsb.org.uk/uk-small-business-statistics.html) state that during that same period ..." between 2021 and 2022 the number of private sector businesses decreased by 86,000 (6%) in England and by 1,000 (<1%) in Scotland, whilst increasing by 11,000 (5%) in Wales and by 4,000 (4%) in Northern Ireland." Food for thought. And well done Wales!

So what do we make of that? I have not had access to data that would enable me to identify the composition in terms of gender of the 86,000 businesses that closed. I am however thrilled to hear about the 140,000 new Female Founders and the 11% increase in SMEs in Wales, which has been my home since 2006.

I am thrilled to have read that the February 2023 Rose Review update reported, that somewhere in the region of 17,500 16- 25 year old females founded new businesses in 2023. That is twenty-two times greater than in 2018. A report by the Federation of Small Businesses on "SMEs and The Economy" (https://www.fsb.org.uk/uk-small-business-statistics.html) states that, "SMEs account for 99.9% of the business population (5.5 million businesses) SMEs account for three-fifths of the employment and around half of turnover in the UK and that half of the business population are solopreneurs..."

In that makeup of SMEs, Female Founded businesses are in the minority. If we are dependent within our economy on SMEs, it makes it even more important to encourage and invest in Female Founders.

It seems that diversity in business is imperative when one looks at the data. I cannot help but begin to understand and to also, make it my mission to convince others that the UK economy demands diversity, inclusion, and all cognitive and innovative talent to thrive! We build together or not at all!

Briana van Strijp, CEO, Anthemis Group (where women comprise 57% of its decision makers and investment team AND 45% of its portfolio companies have founders who are female or of colour) strongly holds to the view that diverse teams are better equipped to outperform the market. I quote her from the Alison Rose Review 2022 update- "research shows that companies who embrace diversity really do achieve better results."

These ideals will remain pipe dreams without backing and investment from Funders. I am pleased to report that a new £22 million fund to support UK female fintech founders was launched after the 2019 Rose Review, in partnership with Barclays. A further £2 billion of ring-fenced funding was announced by NatWest for female entrepreneurs after the Rose Review. A definite start in the right direction.

BAME BUSINESSES

I am pleased that Barclays Bank and Natwest responded to the call for funding for female Founders. But what of the other banks, Funders and Venture Capitalists? How do we bridge the gap between finance and opportunities for the BAME Businesses? How equitable are the measures being used to decide to whom Funding will be given? How do we decide who gets approved for bank accounts and who gets refused? Where are the Mentors and Coaches that share the background, culture colour and beliefs of the BAME, "would be" entrepreneurs?

I was privileged to be invited as an expert panelist at the October 2020 launch of the British Business Bank's Report...Alone Together- Diversity and Entrepreneurship in the United Kingdom. This report covered the entire United Kingdom and the focus was on entrepreneurship and whether or not diversity played a role in how businesses scaled, were sustained, or failed. Not surprisingly, among other things, this report highlighted the stark disparity between BAME businesses and their white counterparts who were less qualified and did not work as hard.

I will insert a snapshot I gleaned from an infographic produced by the British Business Bank, summarising the findings.

"Money plays a vital role- those who are poorer experience less success...

...There are persistent disparities in outcomes for business owners from ethnic minority backgrounds...Black business owners report £25k median turnover vs £35k for White business owners and £40k for Asian and Other Ethnic Minority business owners

38% of Asian and Other Ethnic Minority business owners and 28% of Black business owners report making no profit vs 16% of White business owners

49% of Black entrepreneurs say they met their non-financial aims vs 53% of Asian and Other Ethnic Minority entrepreneurs and 69% of White entrepreneurs

Disparities explained by:

- Access to finance
- Education
- Deprivation
- Under-representation in senior roles
- Systemic disadvantage

Female entrepreneurs from ethnic minority backgrounds experience the biggest disparities

Over 1/3 of Black, and Asian and Other Ethnic minority female business owners report making no profit last year, vs 15% of White female business owners

Irrespective of ethnicity. female business owners experience significantly lower median turnover than male business

Female £15k

Male £45k

Even after accounting for caring roles and part-time work, substantial disparities persist for female entrepreneurs

Location is an important factor in success, irrespective of ethnicity and gender

Only 71% of London business owners reported a profit in 2019- the lowest in the UK

20% of business owners in London saw a decline in revenue last year vs UK average of 14%

12x Business owners with household income of £75k+ have a median turnover 12 times that of those with an income of under £20k

South East based entrepreneurs see the most success with a median turnover of

£35k

49% of Asian and Other Ethnic Minority entrepreneurs cite difficulties getting finance as the reason for stopping work on their business idea"

This snapshot could be seen as throwing up more questions than answers. This too might be the view of my reader so far.

Some of the observations within the report were that there seemed to be no credible reason for the disparities. These BAME business owners were most of the time just as or more qualified than their white counterparts and worked that much harder as well.

One of the points that I made within the discussions on the panel at the launch event was that social capital and the lack thereof was a consideration. The reason is that the majority of BAME businesses are founded by frustrated corporate employees who are not getting the recognition or escalation they think they deserve. They segway into entrepreneurship in response, but they miss some vital steps in development as a result.

These steps are opportunities to network, to meet influential people and develop a network of connections. They remain relatively unknown to influential people. They have not had a chance to learn the art of engagement and other key skills required to be successful as an entrepreneur.

Whilst I am by no means suggesting that Banks, investors, and funders only accommodate their friends, I am of the view that a big part of selling an idea is selling yourself. An entrepreneur needs all the help he or she can get to make it through the door and get the requisite attention and support.

I will be developing on these matters throughout this book and introducing other important topics for thought. Bear with me as I hope that as you journey with me, our hearts and minds might meet. You see, I do believe in this post pandemic economy; the tides are at the flood and the current is served. Let us take it! Let us not be the generation that fails to ride the cusp of this new wave and neglect to exert our influence for deliberate diversity!

"By creating space for diverse groups to display and hone their talent and expertise we allow them to enjoy deserved promotion and escalation. The result is we in turn gain the benefit of disruptive, innovative, and groundbreaking thinking and expertise."

Bernie Davies

INFORMATION BUBBLES & ECHO CHAMBERS

2 INFORMATION BUBBLES & ECHO CHAMBERS

The algorithms used by social media platforms, Google, and Streaming platforms, to allow them to better entertain, inform and inspire us, now imprison us in a virtual "mutual admiration society," developing "crowd immunity" to any views, beliefs, affiliations, sexual and political persuasion which does not align with ours. When we examine how echo chambers are formed, we realise how unwittingly we are complicit in polarising our experience and our thought leadership by ONLY liking, commenting, and sharing what resonates with us AND blocking, ignoring, and unfriending, what and who does not.

As we know, many still credit the Trump election "upset," with this strategy. They assert that his opponents were literally "excluded" from the echo chambers that were backing Trump. The algorithms, they say, "hid" Trump's popularity in feeds to which his detractors were not made privy. I cannot begin to fully back the veracity of this assertion, but I certainly favour this view.

However, how does that "translate" in my world and work? My Google page search results differ from my 30-year-old upwardly mobile daughter's... and hers from her 40-year-old conspiracy theorist brother's on any given topic within the same time stamped search. This is true for us all. You should test it.

I, like my colleagues, am just as vulnerable and have been just as guilty of not commenting, liking, or sharing anything that does not resonate with me. As a result, public figures, government agencies, universities, colleges, banks, and businesses, with whom I interact on social media, are ever prevalent and prioritised on my feeds. I must admit that I only receive and subscribe to newsletters on LinkedIn and Google that share my passion for diversity, female empowerment, Ted Talks, mentoring and publishing. I am inundated with LinkedIn connection requests from Founders, Managing Directors and Large companies with a great entrepreneurship and DEI focus. Surprised? Not really.

Whilst, prima facie, it might seem great, what of the polarisation of my potential client base to only segments of Australia, United States, Europe, and a few key regions in the United Kingdom? I noticed that recently. I realised that the mutual admiration society I had unwittingly formed and chaired over the years was limiting me. I intentionally changed my interactions over a period of 14 days, and I immediately noted a shift...at least on LinkedIn. How can I win converts if I am consistently preaching to the choir?

I mentioned the erudite Chimamanda Ngozie Adiche, in the previous chapter and in particular, her Ted Talk, *"The Danger of a Single Story."* The reason this talk moved me so much and I see it fit to share it with you at this point, is that I am convinced that unconscious based, based on ignorance and suspicion, finds its roots in story telling or stories.

As a child in the Caribbean, I use to watch an interminable amount of broadcasts which were produced by the international press about all parts of the African continent. These programmes showed victims of famine in their most graphic and tragic states. There were and still are films showing flies on eyes that seemed to have forgotten how to blink, bare breasted women of not the flattering type and bellies distended from starvation and not gluttony as we see this side of the world. I remembered in my childhood innocence being grateful for slavery which took me away from that place. I am disgusted by this memory to this day, but I cannot pretend to not myself have been as much a part of the problem, I am now asking you to join me in fixing.

On the flipside, I also saw films which were produced about my country and region, which did not show any beauty beyond the resorts. Nowhere to be seen were the lovely mansions that the vast middle class live in. There was no sight of the incredible infrastructure. And it always puzzled me, when they reported on hurricanes, that the hurricanes seemed to have only hit the slums...because that was where and is STILL where the cameras go. I did not see **my** world EVER reflected in the international press.

Was it any wonder then, that I used to be asked, when I travelled overseas, if we had KFC? Any wonder, when my mother went to the USA in the 1970s she was asked whether we lived in trees?

Mastering Diversity: "We go together or not at all!"

Would it surprise you to find out I had culture shock when I moved to the UK and our first home had ONLY one bathroom? Would it further confuse you that an ensuite bathroom was par for the course for me in the Caribbean? And would the icing on the cake be that despite this, I was not born into a high ranking government family?

In Chimamanda's Ted Talk, she spoke of coming from a financially comfortable background. They had household staff and she too paid scant attention to her staff from the villages. The shock came when she went to study in the USA and she realised that her fellow classmates who clearly watched the same films I did about Africa, were NOT prepared for her. There she was, showing up with modern devices and having the temerity of actually knowing who Britney Spears was…plus having the audacity of owning her CDS!

The best part of her Talk, however, is where she admitted to also being a perpetuator of the "single story." Whilst in the USA Chimamanda visited Mexico and all her unconscious bias and preconceived notions, which were based on the narrative of the international press, came to the fore. She was not prepared to see the wealth, the infrastructure, the civilized society, the pomp, and the fashion. I was challenged by her message and encouraged by her mission to change her sphere of influence by first changing herself. I was proud of the lack of accusations and anger. Too long we have used our swords and now we do the same amount of damage with the pens for which we have traded in our swords.

We navel gaze and we inspire hatred because we are frustrated and we are afraid. But, ironically, this actually perpetuates the single story of those who have not taken the time to know and value us. We need to look outside of ourselves and at the wider issues. As my friend Cody Gapare says, "it is time to get down from our soapboxes and pull up a chair." In other words, it is time to talk, to provide platforms to listen as well as to be heard.

Let us bring it into the Welsh context, as this is now my home and where I concentrate my DEI work. What are the stories that we have been told that inform how we choose our friends, employ, collaborate, invest, sponsor, and support with our time and expertise?

One of the first stories we are told is that strangers are dangerous and we should NOT speak to them. We might "speak" to people from backgrounds, cultures, race, countries, and beliefs which are "strange" to us BUT do we? Do we speak to them with a heart and a mind to give of ourselves in that exchange? Or are we still not REALLY speaking to strangers, as we go through the motions of the language of social cohesion?

It might be interesting to hear what goes through one's mind if he or she is from Swansea and a new team leader joins his or her workplace, from Cardiff. For those who are not familiar with Wales, it would be tantamount to a West Indies Cricket fanatic having to take orders from the English Cricket captain…exactly! That Team Leader would be starting at a disadvantage.

The only way to breakdown unconscious bias is to clear away suspicion. Suspicion can only truly be eradicated with transparency. Transparency will only be possible if all parties feel safe enough to lower their walls and let the other side in. What we fail to realise is that both sides, the victim, and the perpetrator, of unconscious bias and discrimination, are desperately afraid…one of the known and the other of the unknown.

So how shall the twain meet? We need to take advantage of the age in which we now live. Digital technology is king! Social media platforms and AI. I believe that if we are aware of a problem and we are giving it more than a passing glance, the likelihood is we have a part to play in fixing it. We are here for a reason and we are all responsible.

It does not take rocket science to figure out that if the media, social media, and broadcast media have a big part to play in the single stories that feed suspicion, fear, and division, we should use these very means to reverse the "curse."

"So what can I do Bernie? I am just a solopreneur in a big country?"

Solopreneur, entrepreneur, corporate giant, student, or political hopeful…you can still make your difference. The first change you can make is to stop believing that you have all the answers and everyone else is mistaken. We must start from the premise that we are all tainted in one form or another by the "stories" we heard from our parents, schools, places of worship and communities. We therefore need to be prepared to test our beliefs. No need to fear. ALL good beliefs will stand testing.

The second thing is to start searching out varying opinions, with an open mind. You might still return to your original viewpoint, but at least you will be clear about WHY? Remember, the information is only as good as the source and the source is only as good as how well it stands up to scrutiny. Test the source and search many sources.

The third thing is to also to be committed to being a source. Add your narrative to the "stories." Stretch the borders of those echo chambers and burst those information bubbles. Start telling your story…be it work or personal. It is up to you. But bear in mind that hugely successful people gain a great measure of success by letting people in!

In essence, diversify your giving and receiving of information online. Break out of any information bubbles or echo chambers you might find yourself lost in at the moment.

I know they are only small steps…but they are important steps in the right direction, nonetheless. When we interact more with thought leaders on various platforms who might not share our ideals, it keeps us informed and current. Remember, knowledge is power!

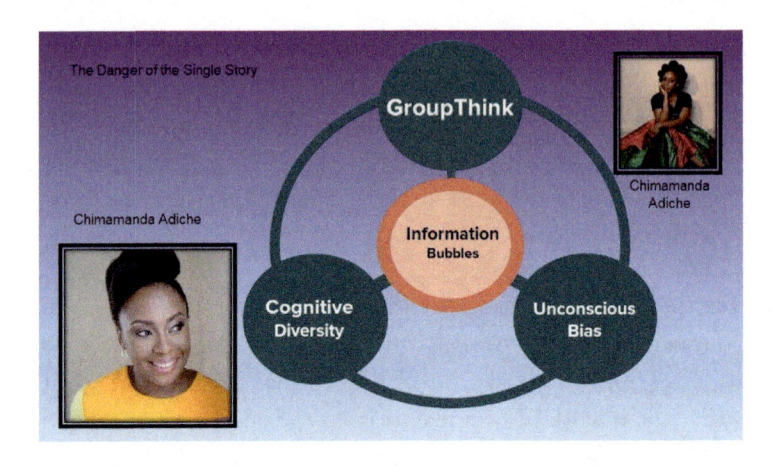

Mastering Diversity: "We go together or not at all!"

"We inadvertently inform the creation of an information bubble that limits our ability to learn, understand or accept anything beyond our own lived and shared experiences with our kind."

Bernie Davies

GROUPTHINK

3 GROUPTHINK

Groupthink and Its Challenges

In a world where there is so much discontent, war, rumours of war, social and political unrest, there is a lot of store set on harmony, being team players and maintaining the status quo. Phrases like "they never have a bad word to say" or "they are so easy going" and "a pleasure to be around" sound the death knell for independent thinking and opinions in a group setting. We think twice about pushing our "heads above the parapet" and be mistaken for troublemakers.

Everyone is quick to cite the ***Bay of Pigs*** incident or the ***Apollo13*** as examples of the potential horrors of Groupthink. However, in the microcosm of our worlds of work and enterprise, we are complicit in perpetuating the spirit of groupthink, dressed up as harmony and team playing.

As influencers and team leaders we reinforce this fear of speaking up, whether inadvertently or on purpose, when we prioritise the views of some over those of others. One example is a team leader always addressing those who look or think like them in meetings and consistently cutting off others, when they are trying to speak.

In the Rose Review 2022 update, Lorna Armitage, and Andrea Cullen Capslock Founders, (who are on a mission to change lives, by offering flexible, inclusive, online cyber skills training with no fees upfront), were commended for speaking out when they were made to feel less important than their male co-Founder in multiple meetings with a potential Funder. And I quote their account within the Rose Review…

"We tracked how often people addressed our co-founder Jonathan rather than us in meetings," explained Lorna. Over eighteen meetings, Andrea was addressed by name 11 times, Lorna 16 times and Jonathan 117 times…However, one of the best things to come out of the situation was that one of our investors saw our report and contacted us to apologise if they had ever prioritised Jonathan's input over ours and promised to be more conscious of this in future. Receiving that email was great."

Admittedly, they risked being labelled and losing their reputation within the Funding community. And yes, they were two out of 3 founders and only one was being prioritised. But Groupthink does not have to be effective with a majority. All it requires to keep others in check, not giving vital opinions or information, and going along with a dangerous plan, is a dominant charismatic figure.

In my line of work, I support teams and entrepreneurship programmes. I work with both the cohorts and the management teams that oversee them. I have been at times in the middle of the emerging needs of the participants and the priorities of the management team. I have seen (and thankfully not too often) where the dominant persona convinces the rest of the management team to stick with a particular plan in the face of new and relevant information. In those circumstances, the end result, if I am unsuccessful in changing minds, is always detrimental to the project objectives. Interestingly, there was also never a real sense of prevailing harmony.

Groupthink and Wales

We are agreed that Groupthink is, "a psychological phenomenon where the pursuit of agreement becomes so dominant in a cohesive group, that it tends to overshadow realistic appraisal of alternative courses of action"[1] (**Janis, 1972**). It severely impacts decision-making processes in organisations[2] and therefore has larger implications for the socio-economic fabric of a region or a country like Wales.

With this in mind, please bear with me as I provide some evidential anecdotes to support my argument that it is important to be aware of Groupthink in our attempts and mastering diversity. By being aware of its subtleties and the fact that it indeed dwells among us, we should be better able to apply the principles, behaviours and strategies necessary to not allow this

---

[1] Janis, I. L. (1972). Victims of Groupthink: A psychological study of foreign-policy decisions and fiascos. Houghton Mifflin.

[2] Turner, M. E., & Pratkanis, A. R. (1998). Twenty-Five Years of Groupthink Theory and Research: Lessons from the Evaluation of a Theory. Organizational Behaviour and Human Decision Processes, 73(2-3), 105-115.

phenomena to negatively impact the socio-economic and political landscape of Wales.

One of the key examples of groupthink in Welsh history dates back to the 19th century when Wales was one of the world's leading coal producers. Coal owners and industrialists failed to diversify into other industries, partly due to groupthink, leading to a near total reliance on coal **(Jones, 1984).** When global coal markets began to decline, the Welsh economy suffered, highlighting the long-term dangers of groupthink.

Fast forward to today, Wales's socio-economic scene largely involves the public sector, agriculture, manufacturing, and a growing digital industry. There have been instances where groupthink has led to flawed strategies, such as in public health decisions. According to a research report by the University of Cardiff (2022), "during the COVID-19 pandemic, the absence of dissenting voices in crisis management committees sometimes led to the adoption of ill-suited strategies that overlooked localised conditions".

Within the burgeoning digital sector, some Welsh companies such as Admiral Group PLC have recognised the dangers of groupthink and have taken steps to foster diversity and encourage dissenting opinions. They believe that "a diversity of perspectives can lead to innovative solutions and better decision-making" **(Admiral Group, 2023).**

That aside, here are some of the ways groupthink still threatens Wales's industries and socio-economic status in several ways as follows:

1. **Homogenised Decision Making:** Groupthink leads to a homogenisation of decisions, stifling innovation and creativity. Pretty much Groupthink does not make room for cognitive diversity. This is particularly harmful for the digital and technology sectors, where innovation is key for growth and staying competitive.

2. **Ignoring External Factors:** As groupthink encourages conformity, it can result in ignorance of or external threats or changes in market conditions, as was seen during the decline of the coal industry. And of course, it plays into information bubbles and echo chambers. One can only look at the recent covid-19 crisis. The businesses that were able to successfully pivot, were the ones who were on top of market trends. They were already, or quickly started to be aware of the global marketplace, the online platforms that they needed to access and the innovation that was available to launch and scale their businesses, in the midst of a global socio-economic shakeup.

3. **Suppression of Dissent:** Groupthink can suppress dissenting opinions and potentially valuable alternative perspectives. This is dangerous in sectors like healthcare, where the quality of decision-making has direct impact on public health.

This threat to diversity and inclusion is especially important and I am not reinventing the wheel or coming up with new ideas. I am simply making information accessible to my readers and adding my perspectives. I am also including synopses of research that has already been done in Wales and encourage you to find the sources for a more detailed reading. We cannot master diversity in a vacuum.

Data on Groupthink and Its Impact on Organisations and Socioeconomic Matters in Wales

In Wales, evidence of groupthink is identified within diverse organisations and sectors. For example, research conducted by Cardiff University (2018) identified groupthink symptoms within the Welsh manufacturing industry[3]. The study suggested that managers were inclined to suppress dissenting opinions, consequently creating an environment that promoted conformity and uniformity. This backs up my previous point about the risks of suppressing dissent.

Similarly, Aberystwyth University (2021) identified instances of groupthink within the Welsh healthcare system, leading to misinformed policies that lacked diverse perspectives[4]. Such instances in both private and public sectors highlight the pervasive nature of groupthink and its potential to compromise effective decision-making. I would also add that the potential disasters that could be averted if Groupthink is contained and diminished, merit a serious campaign against its advancement within Welsh culture.

---

[3] Cardiff University. (2018). The Impact of Groupthink on Organisational Decision-making: A Case Study of the Welsh Manufacturing Industry.

[4] Aberystwyth University. (2021). Groupthink and Its Consequences: A Study of the Welsh Healthcare System.

So how does a culture of Groupthink threaten aspects of Welsh industry and socioeconomic matters, you may ask? By, prioritising consensus over constructive debate and individual innovation, groupthink hampers organisations' competitiveness in a rapidly evolving global economy. For instance, in industries such as technology and manufacturing, homogeneity of thought will prevent Welsh companies from adapting to changes in market conditions or innovating to meet customer needs.

It needs reiterating, that groupthink jeopardises socioeconomic stability. For instance, in public sector decision-making bodies such as health boards or councils, conformity can lead to flawed strategies, such as inefficient allocation of resources, which can negatively impact social welfare. It might not seem to bear repeating, but to be honest, I think I need to state that we tend to look after our own. What do I mean by that? There are several examples that I can give, of Funds being made available for a certain sector of the society and they do not even know that it is there. So, what has that got to do with groupthink? Well, if we are only speaking, collaborating and engaging with those who conform with our ways of thinking, the ones who fall outside of this, will not be any the wiser.

Let us look at the Shared Prosperity Fund for example. As my knowledge of the specifics of how the Shared Prosperity Fund (SPF) was to be implemented in Wales or elsewhere is limited, I will not assert, to be an expert or to be 100% accurate. I am merely sharing my limited knowledge and perspectives. The UK government stated that the SPF was to be used to "level up" and create opportunities across the country, by replacing the EU's structural funds post-Brexit.

It was designed to reduce inequalities within communities, and funding should be targeted towards areas with higher levels of poverty, unemployment, or economic deprivation, communities who are underprivileged or marginalised, including people from BAME backgrounds or lower economic brackets.

However, the specific criteria for SPF allocation, the application process, and the monitoring procedures have not been provided. These details would include how the SPF ensures fair access for BAME communities and individuals from lower economic brackets. The government has stated that the SPF would be aligned with the UK's wider equality objectives. One would assume, this should include stipulations to ensure that the fund is distributed in a way that promotes racial equality and social mobility.

The role of local and regional authorities, including those in Wales, is crucial in the SPF's implementation. Their knowledge of local community needs can help ensure that funding is targeted effectively. It is also expected that local communities will have a say in how funding is used, potentially through public consultations.

Here lies the problem that groupthink introduces. If the decision makers and Fund Managers within the Local Authorities within the UK and Wales, do not encourage a diversity of opinions and considerations, when setting the criteria for access to the SPF, when agreeing the methods of monitoring fair distribution and establishing appropriate ways of making the information about the opportunity accessible to ALL, inequity will result. For example, I know of one particular local authority in South Wales, where applications for the Shared Prosperity Fund are by INVITATION ONLY! How did that decision come about? How do they decide whom should be invited? How will those who need it most be given an invitation to treat?

There needs to be government monitoring and evaluation of the SPF, ensuring that the funds are used effectively and reach the intended beneficiaries. There has to be a way, also, of tracking the outcomes of projects funded by the SPF to assess whether they have succeeded in reducing inequalities and creating opportunities.

The good news is that several Welsh organisations and research institutions are advocating for the promotion of diverse perspectives, healthy debate, and an environment that encourages questioning and critique. Cardiff Business School, for instance, offers training and development programmes to equip leaders with the tools to recognise and combat groupthink[5].

The National Assembly for Wales has also introduced protocols to ensure a plurality of perspectives in decision-making

---

[5] Cardiff Business School. (2023). Combating Groupthink: Developing Diverse and Resilient Leadership.

processes, further reflecting a recognition of the threat posed by groupthink[6].

Wales, being a region of the UK with unique socio-economic conditions and challenges, can ill-afford the pitfalls of groupthink. It is therefore essential for Welsh organisations and policymakers to take proactive measures to prevent groupthink. Encouraging diversity, fostering open communication, and valuing dissenting opinions are some of the ways that this can be achieved.

Only by recognising and combating groupthink can Wales hope to make the most of its potential and ensure the continued growth and prosperity of its people.

---

[6] National Assembly for Wales. (2023). A Plurality of Voices: Ensuring Effective Decision-making in Welsh Governance.

COGNITIVE DIVERSITY

4 Cognitive Diversity

Many of us consider cognitive diversity and diversity and inclusion to be a distinction without a difference, but I beg to disagree. My husband and I are from two completely and diametrically opposed backgrounds, religious upbringing, socialisation, and countries. However, we share similar views, enjoy the same pastimes…even mindless reality TV and could easily finish each other's sentences.

By the same token, those of us who have had the privilege of growing up, living and or working in a multicultural context, will find that invariably they will be able to form meaningful and financially viable engagement with people from diverse backgrounds who think the way they do, hold similar ideals, and adhere to their methods.

The magic really happens when we recruit or include in our teams, people with diverse ethnicities, physical capabilities, religious persuasions, gender, and sexual orientation who also bring a diversity of talent, innovative and disruptive thinking, and bold new ways of solving problems and scaling up.

There are various problems that teams face. One common problem that every team shares is the people problem. And yes, it is easy to "play it safe" and get a bunch of people together who have lived, learnt, thought and problem solved the same. But how effective will that be in this post pandemic economy which has obliterated "same" and "norms"? Plus, the truth is that no two people are the same. The age old saying, "seven brothers, seven different minds," was not coined out of the blue. The problem is that the saying was tinged with some amount of regret and warning as opposed to a celebration of the importance of each of us thinking differently and bringing our unique value to bear on the important things. "Playing it safe" truly happens when we include diverse ways of thinking, problem solving, viewing the world and its challenges, and applying innovative problem solving.

In my work, I mentor entrepreneurs to know themselves and embrace what I call their You Print. By knowing yourself, it puts you in a position of power in life and business and frees you to think critically…in your unique way. The other particularly important complement to this, is valuing others and their differences…understanding the differing personality types…what makes them tick, what are their triggers, what builds loyalty, the "language" they speak and the varied ways in which they work. The DISC personality profiling method is a good place to start.

The benefit of this awareness is being in a position to choose the right people for the team to do the right job alongside personality types that compliment and not conflict. It helps team leaders to understand how to motivate, reward and develop effective teams. The right team member will be tasked with the appropriate aspects of the job and team building exercises will be strategically implemented to facilitate harmony.

How many organisations engage in skills audits and develop skill matrices for their Boards, leadership teams and managers? How many of these organisations place as much emphasis on the personality evaluation aspect of their skills audits? How many skills audits contemplate how their staff responds within meetings, what makes them share, what makes them decide to sit quietly, who will challenge the status quo, who will only speak when asked even if they know the answer. How do you detect and encourage disruptive thinking as this individual might not exhibit disruptive behaviour? How weighted are interview questions in ascertaining cognitions?

Why is this so important? My suggestions are by no means exhaustive, but hopefully they will be instructive and should direct our focus. We should pick from this book what suits. Never swallow anything whole, as they say. Chew on it and see what fits your particular palette.

My view is that prioritising and encouraging cognitive diversity will benefit organisations, business owners, the Third Sector, Charities, and the Public Sector.

Problem-Solving

Studies indicate that teams with a wide range of cognitive abilities tend to be more successful in resolving issues compared to those where members think similarly. The variety in viewpoints and ways of thinking can foster innovation. For example, research conducted by the Harvard Business Review revealed that teams with diverse cognitive abilities are quicker at problem-solving than their less diverse counterparts. The Harvard Business Review article titled "Teams Solve Problems Faster When They're More Cognitively Diverse" discusses research on cognitive diversity and problem-solving. The article was published in March 2017. *(You can access the full article at https://hbr.org/2017/03/teams-solve-problems-faster-when-theyre-more-cognitively-diverse)*

Innovation and Creativity

Cognitive diversity serves as a significant catalyst for innovation and creativity. The blend of various thinking styles can generate a broader spectrum of ideas, leading to more inventive solutions and products. For example, I co-led a Welsh government funded project for 2 years with award-winning Food Entrepreneur, Margaret Ogunbanwo, called Bridging the Gap Between Finance and Opportunity for Black Owned Businesses. This project served a cohort of upwards of 24 participants altogether who were mainly from the Food and drink Industry. I am proud to say that because of the mix of cultures, talents and cognitive diversity, there is about to be launched, an incredibly, never been done before product, using an unbelievable leaf! I am very grateful to BIC Innovation who supported this project and made available experts to research and guide this new innovation into reality. Watch this space.

Enhanced Decision Making

The presence of cognitive diversity improves decision-making processes. A group composed of individuals with diverse thinking styles can challenge each other's preconceptions and biases, resulting in more comprehensive and thoughtful decisions. I recall when I was practicing Law and I was in a senior role at a Law Firm in Bradford. There were a few conveyancers who were not functioning efficiently and not meeting their Key Performance Indicators (KPIs). There was one particular young lady who was very close to disciplinary proceedings being initiated. I thought to myself, *there must be another way*. I was convinced that we were not communicating with her and the team, in a way to allow them to engage with the tasks efficiently. Our methods were one dimensional. I am pleased to say that the management listened to me and allowed me to initiate a training programme. One that allowed for engagement and input from the staff into how best to meet the KPIs. Needless to say, not only did they smash their KPIs, but no one was also lost from the team. Production was exponential and to top it all, I got a significant promotion and pay rise. Credit goes to the Law Firm, who took the time to listen to my way of thinking.

Representation of the Welsh Population

Wales, like many other regions, is characterised by a rich diversity in culture, language, and experiences. By promoting cognitive diversity in organisations and public life, this diversity can be mirrored in decision-making processes, leading to results that more accurately represent and cater to the diverse needs of the

Welsh population. I have had the privilege of supporting many initiatives within Wales such as the launch of black pound day, sitting on the Black History Wales 365 management committee, Advisory Panel Member for the Public Services Ombudsman for Wales, Trustee for FIO Arts Charity which focuses on Global Majority Artists, NED for a global Women's Business Club- being integral in influencing and supporting its launch in Wales, NatWest bank Taskforce on Gender Equality, Black Businesses Matter- an initiative by Ubele on behalf of HSBC, Welsh Government Excelerator Programme, Welsh ICE Female Founders, Cardiff Metropolitan University Centre for Entrepreneurship, Swansea Women in Business- a Swansea University Initiative, and University of South Wales Women's Hub. It is fair to say, that I am at the coal face, as we say in Wales, of all things Diversity and Inclusion. I have also had the opportunity to see what happens when the value of cognitive diversity within the Welsh landscape is overlooked. I am pleased to say that attitudes are changing for the better.

Challenges

There can be difficulties. Whenever people are involved, from different backgrounds, ways of thinking and methods of tackling issues, there is the risk that there will be conflict. It is therefore important to couple the creation of a melting pot that is cognitively diverse, with a very open, accessible, and transparent atmosphere. Motives must be clearly defined and Allyship has to be practiced. If not, differences in thinking styles will lead to misunderstandings. Therefore, it is important for organisations to foster an inclusive culture where diverse perspectives are valued and where there are clear communication and conflict resolution strategies in place.

On a more positive note, Welsh organisations such as The Diversity Trust Wales[7] and The Institute of Welsh Affairs[8] have been conducting research and advocating the importance of diversity, including cognitive diversity. These organisations send the message that a team with varied cognitive approaches to problem-solving is more likely to innovate and adapt to changing market conditions, ultimately driving success. They are taking their beliefs that bit further with their advocacy and that is what we can do with more of in Wales and the wider United Kingdom.

I am pleased to also report that, the software company DevOpsGroup[9], based in Cardiff, has also been a staunch advocate for cognitive diversity in the tech industry. The company believes that by diversifying their teams in terms of thought processes and problem-solving strategies, they will foster a more innovative and dynamic work environment. Their commitment to cognitive diversity has been instrumental in driving their growth and establishing them as a leading player in the tech industry in Wales.

With an industry as diverse as that of Wales, which includes manufacturing, services, tourism, and digital technology, the lack of cognitive diversity can lead to an unrepresentative policy-making process. This may result in policies that do not cater to

---

[7] The Diversity Trust Wales, www.diversitytrust.org.uk.
[8] The Institute of Welsh Affairs, www.iwa.wales.
[9] DevOpsGroup, www.devopsgroup.com.

the diverse needs of different social and economic groups within Wales. For instance, decision-making processes dominated by single-minded perspectives can fail to address issues faced by disadvantaged groups, leading to socioeconomic disparities.

The Equality, Local Government, and Communities Committee of the National Assembly for Wales acknowledges this problem. It has been working to ensure that the voices of people from diverse backgrounds, including those from different cognitive perspectives, are included in policy-making processes.[10]

Inclusion and Belonging

For Wales, embracing cognitive diversity can lead to more representative and effective outcomes for its diverse population. Welsh organisations are recognising and addressing this challenge, understanding that cognitive diversity can be a driving force for their growth and the socioeconomic development of Wales.

However, it is important to manage the challenges associated with cognitive diversity effectively to reap its benefits. This is where inclusion is not merely throwing people together in a great potpourri, but also crafting a glorious patchwork which leads to s sense of belonging! How does one do that?...Introducing.... Allyship!.

---

[10] Equality, Local Government and Communities Committee, National Assembly for Wales, www.assembly.wales.

ALLYSHIP

5 ALLYSHIP

What is Allyship? What is this great solution that I am proposing? Firstly, let me lead with the disclaimer that this is not some high level scientific discovery or piece of work. I am sharing MY understanding and using references to my own experience while harking back to what the experts have also discovered and I have found useful. You should choose to deal with my arguments as just that…arguments to consider and treat with as you see fit. However, I am great believer in learning from other people's mistakes and not reinventing the wheel. "If it ain't broke, don't fix it!" Anonymous

Let us start with the simple Cambridge Dictionary definition of Allyship= "the quality or practice of helping or supporting other people who are part of a group that is treated badly or unfairly, although you are not yourself a member of this group:

One of the most important ways to practise allyship is just to listen."

I could wrap it up here…but I have some pages to fill! In all seriousness, it…IS… that…simple to make an extremely mammoth difference within the workplace and our communities. Just become Allies AND teach others how to do that too.

You will invariably start questioning the simplicity of this assertion, by looking for ways you believe you are powerless to make a real difference or ill equipped to influence the requisite change of attitudes. To some extent you are right in looking at the task as one that requires some power. And, to further quote from the Cambridge dictionary online, "Allyship means using your power, position, or privilege to uplift others."

So let us start at the beginning and look at where we are able to apply Allyship. One of the key places is work and we are most of us, in some form of work. I will therefore use the workplace for my focus in this chapter.

In our workplaces there are hierarchies and there are teams. There is almost always someone who has been there for eons and someone who is just joining. There is someone who is mouthy, the office clown, the quasi bully, the princess, the Boss's pet, the swot, the one that does not quite fit in and so on. Now one of the things that tends to go unnoticed is that these various "positions" were allowed, fostered, and encouraged by those with influence within the workplace. There would not be an office clown if the person managing the teams did not encourage inappropriate banter during working hours. Now, I am the first one for a laugh, but I hope you get where I am coming from.

The office "queen / princess" would not be reigning if this behaviour of quasi- bullying and marginalising others did not go unchecked by leadership. In fact, Leadership creates these demarcations by how they interact with their teams. For example, who are the ones that get recognition and advancement all the time? Is there a fair opportunity given for the not so up front ones to contribute equally to meetings or to get credit for the work they have actually done?

And, on the other hand, what is the reason for the one that does not fit in to be so dubbed? Is it that they are not allowed to? One has to look at all of these attitudes that one can change in one's day to day interactions, chats at the coffee machine or water station and managing group dynamics.

I will quote from industry giant Deloitte where they named 2022, the year of Allyship. They reported this year and I quote…" ***In 2021, to support inclusion, we launched our allyship toolkit, packed with information and ideas to help us all support colleagues from under-represented groups. This year, our Gender Balance Network created the Better Balance Framework to promote gender allyship with tips for leaders on how to be better allies.***

And we're gaining on our goal of having 40 per cent female partners by 2030; in 2022, 35 per cent and 39 per cent of our partner and director promotions were women. Deloitte was once again named a Times Top 50 Employer of Women.[11]

One major allyship achievement this year was the launch of our Neurodiversity Network, supporting and celebrating

---

[11] https://www2.deloitte.com/uk/en/pages/press-releases/articles/deloitte-named-a-top-50-employer-for-women.html

neurodivergent colleagues. We now have 13 diversity networks with thousands of members.

Anthony Friel, Deloitte Neurodiversity Network lead, says, "I felt like I could never succeed anywhere people knew I was neurodivergent; the label always became a way to devalue my perspective and my contribution. Deloitte was the first place I had ever felt I could bring my entire self to work." As part of the launch, we created two learning guides for recruiters[12], aimed at resourcing professionals and businesses. These workbooks will help recruiters develop a better understanding of neurodiversity and the benefits neurodivergent candidates can bring to business.

In November, our Workability Network – a network for anyone at Deloitte with direct experience of a physical disability, chronic ill-health or a mental health condition – as well as carers and allies, hosted a week-long series of events to mark International Day of Persons with Disabilities (#IDPWD – 3 December). This year, the focus was on how to be a better ally and the importance of having conversations around disability, visible or otherwise.

Julie Addis-Fuller, Deloitte Workability Network lead, says, "Our allies are incredibly supportive of people with disabilities, simply by seeing the human. With their help, we're able to encourage a culture where everyone can thrive at work."

---

[12] https://www2.deloitte.com/uk/en/pages/neurodiversity-learning-guides.html

Absolutely remarkable! Deloitte also led "Fast and Curious" which saw non-Muslims join in with Ramadan to show support and in an attempt to understand what they go through every year. These are grand gestures at the world stage level and are very inspiring. However, taken the wrong way, they can make us feel inadequate and redundant in the grand scheme of things. This is the very reason I am motivated to write this book. I am determined to bring allyship up close so you can touch it, pick it up, examine it and see which parts of it you can make a difference in **and** with.

So, what does allyship look like? -

1. Allowing females or marginalised groups or individuals, the same opportunity to contribute to meetings. That means not interrupting them and asking them to "save that for another time", after just giving their white, male, straight or able-bodied counterpart 10 minutes for their contribution about something or nothing

2. Encouraging an inclusive atmosphere in the workplace, where there is opportunity for individuals or groups, to share what affects their sense of belonging, what actions cause them to feel isolated, and what habits of their white, male or able-bodied or straight counterparts, cause them to feel belittled, undervalued and isolated

3. Encouraging and rewarding allyship amongst staff/ employees. That could simply be setting criteria for staff of the month to include, kindness, respect for colleagues, being a listening ear and going the extra mile for those who are struggling to keep up with targets

4. Providing training where necessary. It is my view that ongoing training is vital, and we never cease to learn DEI is a moving target and so keeping up with information and trends is vital to mastering diversity

What does allyship NOT look like? –

1. Making a definitive statement about a direction you would like the team to take and making it clear it was not up for discussion when the "minority" individual attempted to comment. But…. then immediately giving the dominant counterpart the opportunity to question the direction, taking it on board and expressing a willingness to reconsider

2. Gaslighting- meaning asking questions or making statements that are aimed at causing an individual (reporting a certain treatment) to start doubting whether they did in fact get treated that way

3. Staying silent in the face of overt or subtle marginalising acts. The saying, ***silence means consent,*** is not a throw away statement. I have been the victim of silence in the face of abuse, bullying and isolation whilst my loved one just watched and said nothing out of fear. It had the effect of strengthening behaviours as the message to the offenders was that it was Ok. They had tacit collusion. This went on for years and it only changed when one of their own spoke up about the motivations and apologised. Up until then, the attitude was that I was imagining it. It was not really happening

4. Condescending / passive aggressive behaviours-
    a. Touching of a Black woman's hair
    b. Being asked "where do you **really** come from"
    c. "Why did you leave all that sunshine to come here?"
    d. "No need to get emotional or aggressive!" …. OR "I really like you, you are different from the rest"

If I am totally honest, I do sympathise with my white counterparts, who are having to navigate this new world. Sometimes it must feel like you cannot do wrong for doing right. My advice is to open up the channels of discussion. Make more BAME friends. Find out what the real triggers are, as sometimes it is not what you would readily think.

For example, I have no problem being called a "Black woman" …some might. I do, however, get triggered if within 2 minutes of us being introduced, you have to swiftly tell me you do not see colour. Then I get to hear how many black friends you had in school. Firstly, we are NOW talking about the thing you apparently do not see. I am obliged to give you that very grateful smile that says, "Thank you for your acceptance," when I really want to ask you, "how can you truly get to know ME (and what that means) if you do not blinking see MY colour, like?!" (Spoken in a Welsh Valleys twang)

And before I start getting shouted at, I get it. It is a minefield. ***It's hard like***…as we say in Wales. This is why we are taking this journey together.

So, the alternative? Instead of making sweeping declarations, ask questions that you would ask anyone else. Share a bit about your hobbies, your interests, and your work. Those are safe conversation starters. Ask them the same. Give them a compliment. There MUST be something and if all else fails…you got it…there is always the weather.

In the next chapter, we will take it back to the workplace. In the workplace we have to understand the positional power that some of us wield. We must consider the inequities that exist, as demonstrated in the Allyship Framework diagram and we must zero in on our privilege. This is where I am going to break some beliefs and probably lose some of you. But stay with me. Hopefully, by the end we will see a lot more clearly…together.

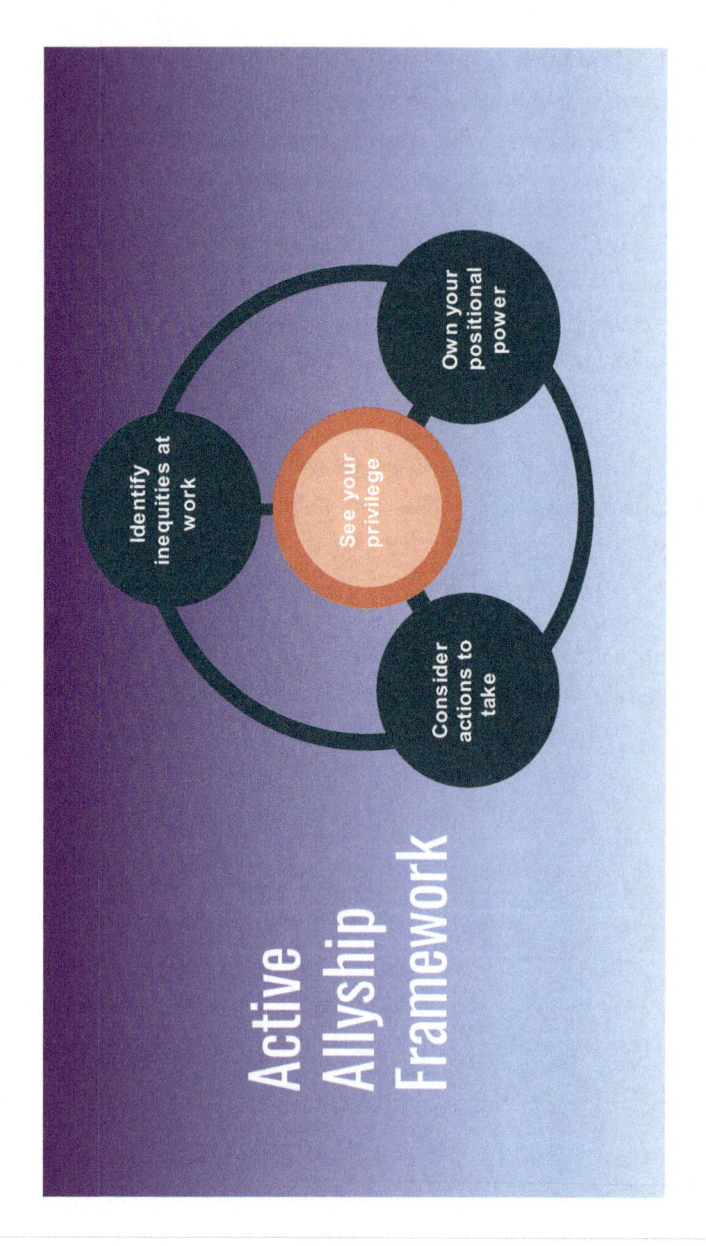

Mastering Diversity: "We go together or not at all!"

Active Allyship Framework

- See your privilege
- Own your positional power
- Identify inequities at work
- Consider actions to take

"It is impossible to apply true and effective Allyship without first coming to terms with our privilege and the latent power we have within us to be changemakers!"

Bernie Davies

PRIVILEGE

6 PRIVILEGE

There is a belief, to which I also hold that says, "the mind of man, once expanded cannot assume its original position."

As a result, I am on a mind expansion mission to-

- Expand the mind to think beyond our own lived experiences
- Expand our minds to ask ourselves, "is this the same for my fellow traveller? And if not, why not? And more importantly "how can I help to change that"
- Expand our minds from "crowd immunity" to the inequalities that exist- think independently of our cliques…family values…negative influencers and selfish ambitions
- Expand our minds to become the change by embracing true allyship

So where do we start? I invite you to look at the little exercise and indulge me by giving it a go. I use this exercise whenever I do Allyship Talks and workshops, as it quickly let us recognise our privilege and as by extension, our resultant responsibilities. I realised that I enjoy privileges over white, blonde women who are obese, I have privilege over 40 something white men who are disabled or have an alternative sexual orientation. I enjoy privilege over my own white counterparts who do not share my social background and are not as educated and connected as I am.

I remember one of my workshops at the 2023 Resilience and Reinvention Conference for one of Wales's largest Gender Equality Charities, Chwarae Teg. I was privileged to be a keynote speaker and then to deliver a more intimate workshop on Allyship. I did the exercise and as I always do, I asked people to indicate how many ticks they had that would confirm their level of privilege. As usual, as in any culturally mixed workshop, there were a lot more white people standing at the end of the exercise than their BAME counterparts. Meaning they had 3 or less indicators of privilege, as far as this particular exercise is concerned. I pointed this fact out as I usually do. And I was pleased that as usual there were more white people standing, *I have made my point,* I thought. I proceeded to explain the importance of not making assumptions about privilege and understanding the many intersections of privilege.

As I progressed the workshop a graceful hand slid timidly up in the back row. And then, an almost childlike voice shakily said, "Bernie can I stop you? I have not heard anything since you did that exercise. So, can I ask you what happens if you could not put even one tick? I could not put any ticks." The tears rolled freely down her face.

Well, that did it did it for every one of us. There was not a dry eye in the room I had to stop. I had to usher her up to the front and I had to give her room to speak…to share what she had been through. It was a moving moment for us, and I will never forget it.

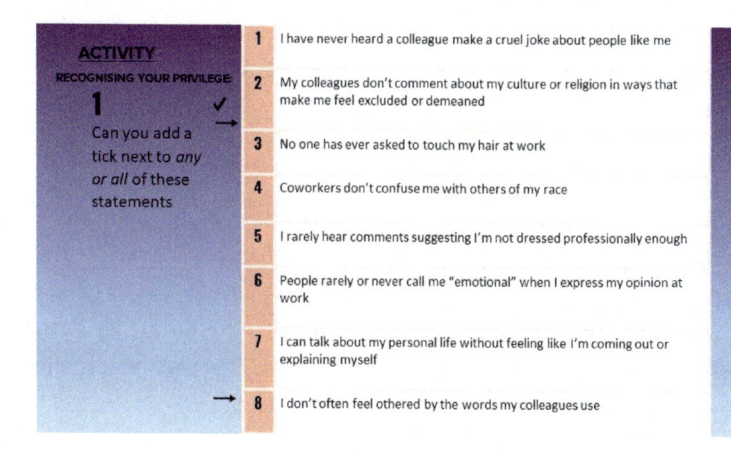

ACTIVITY
RECOGNISING YOUR PRIVILEGE

1 ✓

Can you add a tick next to *any* or *all* of these statements

1	I have never heard a colleague make a cruel joke about people like me
2	My colleagues don't comment about my culture or religion in ways that make me feel excluded or demeaned
3	No one has ever asked to touch my hair at work
4	Coworkers don't confuse me with others of my race
5	I rarely hear comments suggesting I'm not dressed professionally enough
6	People rarely or never call me "emotional" when I express my opinion at work
7	I can talk about my personal life without feeling like I'm coming out or explaining myself
8	I don't often feel othered by the words my colleagues use

Let us take a "deep dive" into Privilege! Simply put, it is the unearned advantages conferred on some individuals by virtue of their race, gender, class, sexual orientation, ability, or other aspects of their identity. It is an important consideration in the context of diversity, equality, and social justice. In this chapter, we will explore the concept of privilege, its place within organisations in Wales, and how the lack of understanding of our privilege and not coming to terms with our power, threatens industry and socio-economic matters.

White Privilege

In "White Privilege: Unpacking the Invisible Knapsack," Peggy McIntosh explores the concept of privilege, focusing primarily on the racial dimension (1988)[13] cites white privilege as an "invisible package of unearned assets" that white people can count on cashing in each day, but about which they are "meant to remain oblivious." This definition is easily transferrable to other aspects of identity as well. For example, gender (male privilege), class (wealth privilege), and ability (able-bodied privilege).

McIntosh postulates that, "white privilege is like an invisible, weightless knapsack of special provisions, maps, passports, codebooks, visas, clothes, tools, and blank checks." As a white person, she was taught about racism as something that puts others at a disadvantage but was never meant to see its underbelly — white privilege, which puts her at an advantage.

She goes on to list fifty everyday benefits of white privilege that she can count on, which non-white individuals cannot. These range from being able to find housing in an area that she can afford and in which she would want to live, having her voice heard in a group in which she is the only member of her race, to being assured that her failures will not be attributed to her race.

McIntosh was on a mission and advocates for more acknowledgment of this unearned privilege and a willingness to reduce or ideally eliminate these unfair advantages. Her hope, and

---

[13] McIntosh, P. (1988). White Privilege: Unpacking the Invisible Knapsack.

mine is that recognition will lead to change...that of the underlying social system that creates them.

Privilege in the Context of Wales

I always like to lead with the good news. I am not trying to set myself up on some moral DEI high ground. I cannot dare to even contemplate, peering down my glasses, with accusatory glares whilst wagging the DEI finger at, "you who need to learn!" All I am trying to do in this book is to speak of my own experiences. Hence, I continue to limit most of my research and anecdotes to Wales. This is where I faced my own fair share of racial abuse, unconscious bias and exclusion. This is also where I enjoyed wide open acceptance and at one point- for a VERY long time- no closed doors! I know that's a contradiction, but that is my true lived experience in this beautiful country I now call home. I hope that my experiences, case studies and research will inspire more people to engage with DEI. I invite more people to do their own research, share their own stories so we can develop a collectively workable plan, which will affect the change we seek.

To that end I am pleased to share that in Wales, the recognition of privilege and efforts to promote diversity have been embraced by various organisations. Here's how:

1. **Organisations and Initiatives**: Many Welsh organisations, including the Equality and Human Rights Commission in Wales, have recognised the importance of understanding privilege and promoting diversity.

Organisations like Chwarae Teg[14], Women's Equality Network[15], and BAWSO[16] are working towards gender equality, providing insights and initiatives for companies to follow.

2. **Government Policies**: The Welsh Government has developed policies to promote diversity, such as the Equality Act 2010. It provides a legal framework to protect the rights of individuals and promote equal opportunities for everyone. Then there is the Anti-Racist Wales Action Plan (first launched in June 2022)[17] and the Criminal Justice- Anti- racism Wales Action Plan (December 2022)

3. Minister for Social Justice and Welsh Government Chief Whip, Jane Hutt, declared when she received her CBE for the Kings Birthday Honours, ***"SEEKING social justice, fairness and equality continues to be at the heart of my work".***

4. Some argue that the plans and programmes implemented by governments throw up more questions than answers. There is news of plans to build an anti-

---

[14] https://chwaraeteg.com/
[15] https://wenwales.org.uk/
[16] https://bawso.org.uk/en/
[17] https://www.gov.wales › anti-racist-wales-action-plan
17 Jan 2023 — What we are going to do to make Wales anti-racist. Part of: Equality planning and strategy (Sub-topic). First published: 7 June 2022.
Criminal Justice Anti-Racism Action Plan for Wales

racism trade union movement where black recruits will thrive.[18]

5. At the same time £4.5M is allocated for culture, heritage and sport actions of the Anti-racist Wales Action Plan. [19]Whilst in other news, at the dawn of 2023, France is accused of its ant-racist action plan denying institutional racism[20] and the UK ant- racism police team is accused of racism[21]. Very curious, perplexing and disheartening. But we must perforce, **keep calm and carry on**…or must we?

6. **Educational Institutions**: Universities like Cardiff University have research centres focused on social justice, equality, and diversity. They provide research, education, and consultation on these matters, helping organisations understand and address issues related to privilege. According to Ethnicity Facts and Figures Services UK BAME students do not do as well at university compared with their White counterparts – the latest statistics show a 13% attainment gap. I googled "What are the statistics on black education in the UK?" I found data that in 2021, the entry rates for all ethnic groups were higher than in the previous year – they were

---

[18] https://www.tuc.org.uk/research-analysis/reports/action-plan-build-anti-racism-trade-union-movement

[19] https://www.gov.wales/funding-announced-culture-heritage-and-sport-actions-anti-racist-wales-action-plan

[20] https://www.hrw.org/news/2023/02/06/frances-anti-racism-action-plan-ignores-institutional-racism

[21] https://www.hrw.org/news/2023/02/06/frances-anti-racism-action-plan-ignores-institutional-racism

also higher than in 2006 (the first year covered by this data) between 2006 and 2021, black pupils had the biggest entry rate increase out of all ethnic groups, from 21.6% to 48.6%

Organisations like Diversity and Anti-Racist Professional Learning (DARPL) [22] as per Welsh Government (2023) statement, "is essential to realising the Curriculum for Wales as it provides high quality resources and opportunities for challenge and support as part of the National Professional Learning Offer", are making an impact in Wales. As are BAMEed Wales Network [23], a national grassroots voluntary network aimed at ensuring our diverse communities in Wales are represented and grow as a substantive part of the education workforce in Wales. Their stated aims are to and sustain change in education. There are several others that could be mentioned. However, this is only meant to be a pocket companion.

Impact on Industry and Socio-Economic Matters

The lack of understanding of privilege has significant implications for both industry and the wider socio-economic landscape in Wales.

Workplace Inequality: When privilege is not recognised, it leads to discrimination and inequality within the workplace. For example, the gender pay gap in Wales continues to be a

---
[22] https://darpl.org/
[23] Contact info@bameedwales.org

significant issue, despite efforts to address it- Office of National Statistics (ONS, 2020)[24].-

1. "Median gross weekly earnings for full-time adults working in Wales were £598.1 in April 2022. This was 93.5% of the average for the UK (£640.0). Median gross weekly earnings in Wales were the eighth highest amongst the 12 UK countries and English regions"[25].

2. The Gender pay gap for women over 50 in Wales is significantly wider- 21%. This was revealed in a 2023 Report by Chwarae Teg, which asserted, "The intersection of different characteristics – age, gender, disability or ethnicity – is resulting in discrimination. Nearly half of women who reported discrimination based on sex/gender also experienced age-related discrimination. Experiencing discrimination in the workplace has a huge impact on women's wellbeing and confidence."

---

[24] Office for National Statistics (ONS). (2020). Gender pay gap in the UK.
[25] https://www.gov.wales/annual-survey-hours-and-earnings-2022

Gender pay difference in Wales by year (median hourly earnings full-time employees excluding overtime) (£) 1997 to 2022

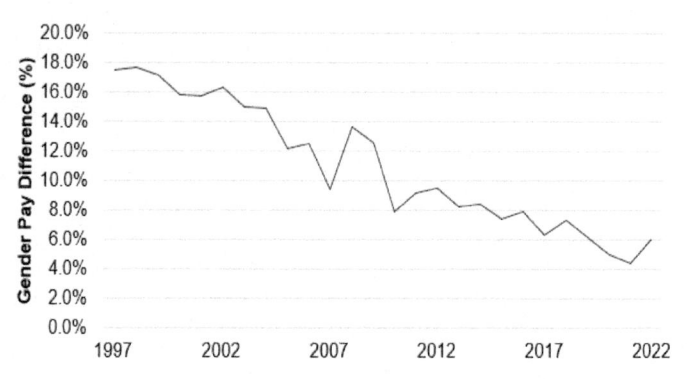

Source: Welsh Government analysis of Annual Survey of Hours and Earnings (ASHE)

1. Median gross weekly earnings for full-time adults working in Wales increased by 6.1% between 2021 and 2022, compared to a 4.1% increase between 2020 and 2021.

2. Median full-time weekly earnings for those living in Wales increased by 5.4% (to £603.5) over the year. The level in 2022 was 94.3 % of the UK average.

Economic Disparities

Lack of recognition of privilege can lead to the perpetuation of socio-economic disparities. Research in Wales indicates that minority ethnic groups are more likely to live in poverty (Joseph

Rowntree Foundation, 2019) [26]. So where are the BAME communities represented in these figures cited above? How do we get more BAME people gainfully employed in areas of their expertise? There is the misconception that BAME communities are bereft of talent and skills required for industry above menial positions. Of course, there is no data to prove that.

Threat to Social Cohesion

The failure to understand and address privilege can lead to division and tension among different social groups. It threatens social cohesion and can even lead to social unrest. "82% of people in England and Wales are white, and 18% belong to a Black, Asian, mixed or other ethnic group" (2021 Census data). BAME community are undoubtedly in the minority but remain an integral part of the societal fabric.[27]

---

[26] **Joseph Rowntree Foundation. (2019). Poverty rates among ethnic groups in Wales.**

[27]

Equality and Human Rights Commission in Wales. (n.d.). Equality Act 2010.
Chwarae Teg. (n.d.). Achieving Gender Equality in Wales.

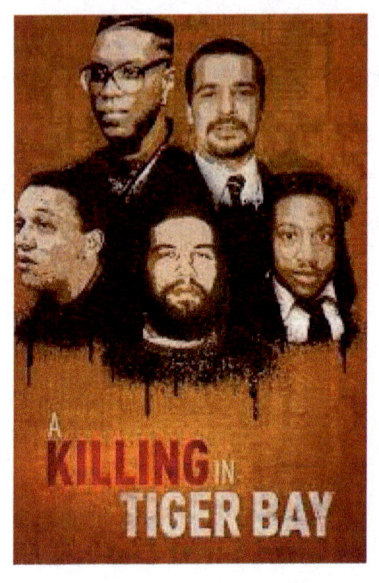

One cannot help thinking about the now famous, unfortunate, "Cardiff 5" who were victims of a society's lack of understanding of privilege and unconscious bias. The flagrant denial of the fact that the policing does not always consider the fact that witness reports and methods of investigations can be coloured by people's biases, led to a gross injustice in February 1988. As a result of ignoring these and many other factors, 5 innocent men were arrested, imprisoned and their lives ruined for a murder they were not even in the room, to have had the opportunity to commit. I will not go into this in detail as I am no expert on it. However, it would be remiss of me to not mention their names. Wales Online report, September 10, 2021, mentioned the "five Black and mixed-race men - John Actie, Tony Paris, Yusef Abdullahi, Ronnie Actie and Stephen Miller- were wrongly accused of her murder, despite a prime suspect being a white man seen crying and covered in blood in the doorway of 7 James Street, where Lynette was killed."

These 5 men did not have the "privilege" of the basic human right of the Rule of Law, innocent until proven guilty. They were deemed guilty before they even had a chance to defend themselves, and by all accounts, even after being totally exonerated, lived, and continue to live with a shadow of suspicion from their white counterparts.

These attitudes lead to a fractious society at best and conflicting groups at its worst, resulting in unrest and even violence.

Given its distinct cultural heritage and increasingly diverse populace, in Wales, understanding and identifying privilege is pivotal. Research by the Equality and Human Rights Commission (2022) highlights stark socio-economic disparities between ethnic groups in Wales. For instance, Black and Asian individuals are more likely to experience unemployment or have lower incomes than their white counterparts. The report implies that these disparities arise due to underlying privileges inherent within the social structures of Wales.

My Research Findings

Companies like Admiral Group, a FTSE 100 company based in Cardiff, have made a concerted effort to address privilege. Their inclusion strategy acknowledges the benefits of diverse perspectives and creates an environment where everyone feels valued, irrespective of their background (Admiral Group, 2023). More people are beginning to realise that "recognising privilege in a professional setting promotes diverse and inclusive workplaces, enhancing creativity, performance, and employee satisfaction" (Hunt, Layton & Prince, 2015).

The Welsh government has recognised these threats. In its Strategic Equality Plan, it emphasises the need to reduce socio-economic inequalities and promotes inclusive and fair workplaces (Welsh Government, 2022). The Welsh Research and Innovation Network also supports projects that address societal challenges, including privilege and inequality (WRIN, 2023).

In summation, organisations and institutions in Wales are making strides to acknowledge and address these issues, but continued efforts are required to ensure equality for all citizens.

References:

- Johnson, A.G. (2006). Privilege, Power, and Difference. McGraw-Hill Education.
- McIntosh, P. (1989). White Privilege: Unpacking the Invisible Knapsack. Independent School.
- Equality and Human Rights Commission (2022). Is Wales Fairer? The state of equality and human rights 2022.
- Chwarae Teg (2023). Equality and Diversity Training.
- Hunt, V., Layton, D., & Prince, S. (2015). Diversity Matters. McKinsey & Company.
- Admiral Group (2023). Diversity and Inclusion Strategy.
- Rock, D., & Grant, H. (2016). Why Diverse Teams Are Smarter. Harvard Business Review.
- Welsh Government (2022). Strategic Equality Plan.
- Welsh Research and Innovation Network (2023). Diversity and Inclusion in Research.

BRIDGING THE GAP AND USING YOUR POWER

7. BRIDGING THE GAP- Use Your Power

If we step back for a moment from statistics, research findings and data and just take a commonsense perspective on what we are observing, we will realise that it is not as complicated as it appears at first glance. Why do we usually find a disconnect between intention and results? The number one reason (certainly as it relates to marriages, for example) is inadequate communication and wrong assumptions. This is also exactly what is one of the main reasons workplaces and communities fail to actually bridge the gap amongst community groups or teams. Nobody takes the time to effectively communicate with the group or individuals they have committed to support. Nobody asks *them* what is that they need to feel included. The people in authority tasked to solve the DEI issues, sit, and talk amongst themselves and conjure up ideas that make THEM feel included. They apply them, create policies that entrench them within their work culture, with no reference whatsoever, to the people they are created for.

It is like the husband who looks forlorn after his wife has left him and says, "I did everything to make her happy. I do not understand." Of course, it usually turns out, he never once asked if her idea of fun was skittles night every Friday with his mates OR he finally realises she was serious when she said, "I cannot cope with your constant golf anymore"

Good Allies use their power to influence others to listen to those who need to feel included and reward and monitor behaviours to ensure allyship is sustained. A couple studies by Leanin and Mckinsey, reflected in the diagrams in this section show how employers in America got it so wrong when they thought they were providing allyship to women of colour. I find it interesting that 77% of white employers saw themselves as allies to women of colour, but less than half of this 77% took the time to educate themselves about experiences of women of colour, even less publicly gave credit to the ideas of women of colour. In the same sample almost two thirds of them did any work to confront discrimination when observed, only 21% advocated for new opportunities for women of colour and a sad 10% only, mentored this group.

Having regard to the fact that the key indicators or imperatives for achieving real allyship, was not being practiced by a collective average of one third of those who asserted that they did, is it any wonder that the divide subsists?

There's a gap between intent and action

White employers...

ALLYSHIP ACTIONS

- 63% (2020) / 77% (2021) See themselves as allies to women of colour
- 45% Educate themselves about the experiences of women of colour
- 43% Publicly give credit to ideas women of colour for their
- 39% Work to confront discrimination when they see it
- 21% Advocate for new opportunities for women of colour
- 10% Are mentoring women of colour

Employees with traditionally marginalized identities are not getting the allyship they deserve

- 63% WHITE — White employees that see themselves as allies to women of colour
- 16% LATINAS / 11% BLACK WOMEN — Employees that think employees of their race and gender have allies at work

LeanIn.Org and McKinsey & Company, *Women in the Workplace 2020* (September 2020), https://womenintheworkplace.com

Intersectionality

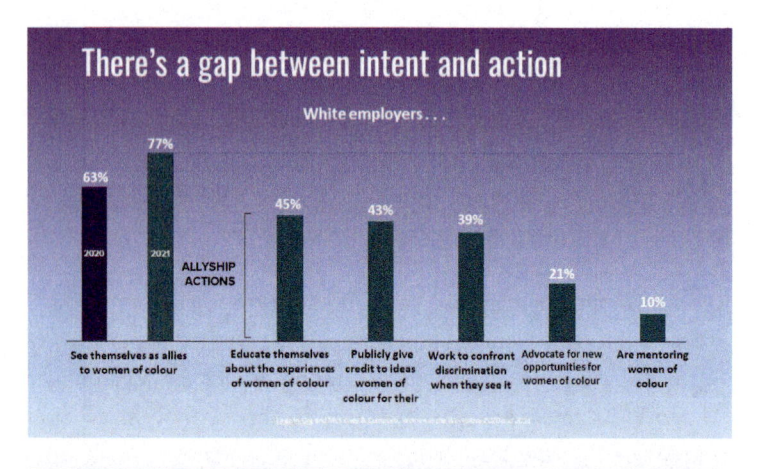

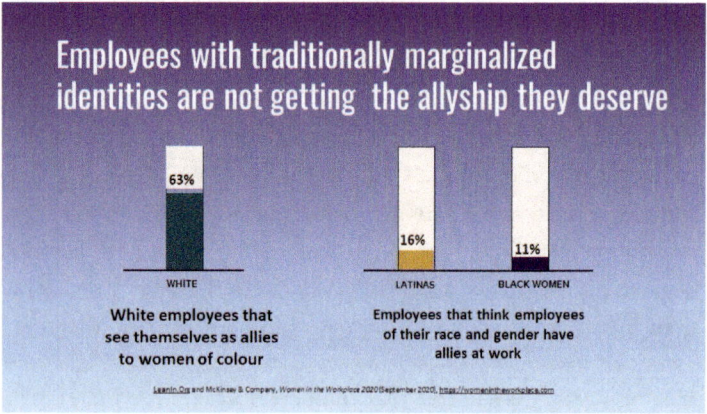

Intersectionality, a term first coined by legal scholar Kimberlé Crenshaw in 1989, refers to the interconnected nature of social segments such as race, class, and gender, which result in overlapping and interdependent systems of discrimination or

disadvantage. An intersectional approach considers that these identities do not exist separately from each other but are interwoven and mutually influence one's experience of the world.

Intersectionality in a Welsh context would consider the various intersections of identity that are unique to Wales, such as race, ethnicity, language (Welsh vs. English speakers), socio-economic class, and rural vs. city living conditions.

The 2011 Census in Wales revealed that 96% of the population identified as white (including Welsh, English, Scottish, and Irish), while 4% identified as Black, Asian, Mixed, or Other (BAME). However, it's important to note that these broad categories can mask the diversity within them. For example, the experiences of a Bangladeshi woman in Cardiff, south Wales, may differ significantly from a Polish man in Wrexham, north Wales.

I will go a bit further to personalise by saying a Black woman like me, who is educated and confident, with a very global experience and outlook will have my own sets of challenges in breaking the glass ceiling maybe. But certainly not the same challenges as a Black woman from a lower socioeconomic background, who does not have tertiary education, is partially sighted and grew up with only the life experience gained from living in a small Welsh village. I hope this makes it clearer.

It is particularly important to gain clarity around intersectionality in any context and in particular in work. The reason for this is we cannot simply "look" at how our teams present and begin to believe we understand the DEI characteristics that present themselves. This is why we need to have conversation, encourage 360 feedback and consistently train our staff.

To quote Kimberlé Crenshaw, "There is no such thing as a single-issue struggle because we do not live single-issue lives." This rings true within the Welsh context where language, ethnicity, and economic class often overlap to create unique experiences of marginalisation or privilege.

For example, the Welsh language, often associated with a national and cultural identity, intersects with other aspects of identity. Being a Welsh speaker might bring certain privileges in predominantly Welsh-speaking areas, but it can also result in disadvantages in areas where English is dominant. These dynamics can further intersect with ethnicity and class, as BAME individuals who are also Welsh speakers may experience unique challenges not faced by their white counterparts.

There is no question that understanding intersectionality in Wales must perforce, play a pivotal role in addressing systemic inequalities and social injustice.

As Bethan Jenkins, a former Welsh Assembly Member, noted, "Unless you reflect modern Wales, you can't possibly hope to represent modern Wales." A quote like this underscores the importance of recognising and addressing intersectionality in creating inclusive policies and social systems in Wales.

On the other hand, however, addressing intersectionality is not just about understanding individual identities but also about understanding the systemic factors and social structures that produce and perpetuate inequalities. It requires urgent attention to ensure that policies, programs, and initiatives do not inadvertently perpetuate these inequalities but rather work towards achieving social justice and equity for all.

To quote Kimberlé Crenshaw once more on intersectionality and women, "When we don't pay attention to the margins, when we don't acknowledge the intersection, we not only fail to see the women who fall outside the parameters of our social justice projects - we fail to see that our efforts are often undermined by the exclusions." This statement underlines the urgency and importance of addressing intersectionality, not just within Wales, but in every context.

The more we understand and treat intersectionality in Wales, we will find that we will develop more effective policies and strategies that address the specific needs and challenges of diverse groups, thereby promoting social justice, equality, and a more inclusive society.

REPRESENTATION
BEING SEEN AND HEARD

8 REPRESENTATION - Being Seen and heard

The State of Diversity in Welsh Politics

Historically, Welsh politics was dominated by a homogenous group of individuals. Over the past couple of decades, there has been an increasing push towards diversifying the representation in the Senedd and local councils. Efforts have been made to increase gender diversity, ethnic representation, and include members from different socio-economic backgrounds.

What Happens When We Feel We Are Not Being Represented

This Linkedin Post demonstrates what can result from consistent feelings of underrepresentation:

"THIS is why I DO NOT and WILL NOT ever subscribe to DEI as a business unit, function, organizational department, or corporate entity.

I'M NOT going to CONVINCE you, EDUCATE you, have an "uncomfortable conversation" or present a business case for you to LEARN how to treat me fairly with the equity, consideration, and respect that are MINE.

YOU cannot give ME anything. How dare you! YOU owe ME! We don't owe you a damn reading list or full-fledged debate to argue for our humanity. GTFOH

The audacity of that repulsive premise and the fact that we've been going along with it; pleading for an opportunity to PROVE we are equal, is so ludicrous that it literally makes me nauseous.

And to add insult to injury, a BILLION dollar DEI industry has been created to capitalize on Black pain, all while telling us not to make everything about race.

Meanwhile, our young men are being killed for EXISTING and dancing with joy. And walking with Skittles and Ice Tea. And jogging through a neighborhood. And selling loosies. And playing with toy guns. And supposedly "whistling" at a girl, who's very much alive in her 80s, while his mother had to bury him in an open casket to show the depravity of racism. But it doesn't matter how many mangled bodies we show you.

YOU DON'T CARE. Then the nerve to GASLIGHT us that WE are violent, lazy, divisive, demanding, intimidating, incompetent, ignorant, hateful and ungrateful.

We did not kidnap 12.5 million PEOPLE who were minding their own business, lie to them and the rest of the world that you found subhuman monkeys in the jungle fit for nothing else but to build your country from the ground up for 250 years of legalized FREE labor, murder with

INSURANCE payouts for killing us because we were YOUR property, and legal rape of men and women, while breeding us like a science experiment.

That was followed by 100 years of segregation because The Supreme Court of the United States ruled that "Separate but Equal" would become the law of the land in 1896.

That meant we were NOT ALLOWED LEGALLY among you for 100 years.

No schools, businesses, parks, hospitals, hotels, or restaurants. We were OUTCASTS in America for 100 years until Brown vs. Board, argued by Thurgood Marshall, struck the doctrine down in 1954.

Do YOU know history? My Dad was born in 1942, a year after Emmit Till. Rather than history, this is the present day because we have so many hashtags for our young Black boys that we can't keep up with them all.

Yet, you tell us NONE of that matters and we should "pull ourselves up by our bootstraps" because YOU DO NOT CARE about the immoral cost of what has been done to us.

And, that is DISGUSTING!! 🤮

Do not argue with me, debate me or come for me when I did not call you. Scroll by or your comments will be deleted and you will be blocked.

I've already blocked TWO Whataboutism Warriors. You've been warned. And, no I'm not interested in "dialogue" about basic human dignity.

Have a blessed and peaceful Sunday. 🙏"- Elizabeth Leiba- Author of Amazon Bestseller, I'm Not Yelling: A Black Woman's Guide to Navigating the Workplace. Seen in NY Times, Forbes, Entrepreneur, Bloomberg & TIME Magazine - LinkedIn Top Voice

Some of us might read this rant and roll our eyes in disgust. We might ask, "what on earth possesses people like this, to think that they can rant and rave and cast accusations make sweeping statements incite anger and act as if they are the only ones that matter?"

I remember I was very intolerant of people who spoke like that…living in Jamaica, and not really feeling in any way marginalised. Yes, I have said that I have been bullied and I have felt that I didn't fit in. But it was not acute, and it did not go to my sense of belonging. I did not feel truly that I did not belong in the community or in my world that I called home. It was more a matter of not being able to run with the cool kids because of the way I was being brought up and the fact that I was so obnoxious that not many people wanted to be my friend. I am just being honest.

But, think about any people, as this rant actually reflects, who have always felt underrepresented or not represented at all. A people who feel that the injustices that had been meted out over and over again, have fallen on deaf ears, blind eyes and are entrenched and reinforced by the powers that are supposed to help and relieve the pain. Then what do you say to such a people?

When you think about what the real CRY is, when you pull back the curtains of the rant above…the real cry is the call to be heard. The real cry is to feel represented. The real cry is to see the needs, the rights, issues that affect a group of people, and a nation entrenched in the law. They want to see it reflected in the makeup of government officials. They want to see it in the makeup of the judiciary and the Senedd (in the Welsh context), in the Houses of Assembly, in the House of Commons in the House of Lords…in the places that truly matter.

I remember when I had the privilege of hearing Levi Roots speak at a launch event for the Welsh government accelerator programme in 2020. I was privileged to have been one of the three business coaches that supported a cohort of 20 something upcoming businesses- female entrepreneurs, people from the BAME community, young entrepreneurs under 25…in fact entrepreneurs who were from the underrepresented segments of Welsh society. The project was aimed at helping them to launch or scale up these businesses to £2 million businesses and at least ten members of staff within two years. A very admirable objective and I am pleased to say that quite a few of these businesses have gone on to do incredible things. But this is not what I would like to focus on at this point.

What I would like to focus on is Levi Roots' admission that when he was young in Brixton, he saw nobody that looked like him, that would come into schools and speak to the young people, and to encourage the young people that they can do well. He did not see himself in anyone that was doing anything that mattered. So, he took it upon himself to be one of those who have broken through the glass ceiling and have made an incredible success of themselves, to reach out within the communities, be that representative, be that voice. be that mentor and be that one that speaks for those who do not have a voice.

This is why we need more organisations like the Women's Equality Network in Wales who have launched a successful award-winning campaign diverse 5050 which is all about increase in representation in the Welsh Senedd for women- Equal Power Equal Voice is their mission and an actual mentoring programme. Equal Power Equal Voice supports all women to find their place in government, to provide that representation and to lead that charge to make representations on behalf of their communities. Without that kind of representation how will the true needs of a people be considered? How will these needs be recognised and provided for if the representatives and decision makers have no clue about what truly obtains?

My view therefore, is that we need to have more representation that looks, speaks, thinks and reflects the true components of any society. And yes, in Wales and the United Kingdom in general, the BAME community are in the minority, so one would say, "well if they are in a minority wouldn't the minority ration in the Senedd be a fair representation?"

A seemingly fair comment but it is fundamentally flawed. The question should be, "how many seats are there in the Senedd?" There are 60 seats within the Welsh Assembly. In a report on the

2021 Welsh Election and how diverse the sixth Senedd is[28] it was revealed that, "There are now 26 women Members of the Senedd (43% of all Members), and 34 men. Natasha Asghar MS is the first woman of colour ever to be elected to the Senedd. Her late father Mohammad Asghar was the first Member from an ethnic minority to be elected back in 2007.

The 26 women elected to this 2021 Senedd is slightly higher than the 25 women elected in 2016. However, it is lower than at the end of the Fifth Senedd – where membership changes led to 29 women and 31 men being Members of the Senedd prior to the 2021 election. Of these numbers, there are only 3 members of the Welsh Senedd that identify as BAME.

Diagram of diversity of 2021 Elections

---

[28] https://research.senedd.wales/research-articles/election-2021-how-diverse-is-the-sixth-senedd/

Mastering Diversity: "We go together or not at all!"

The said report revealed that, "*In total, **470 candidates stood for election to the Senedd in 2021**. Of these 322 (69%) were men and 148 (31%) were women. Of the constituency candidates, 220 (71%) were men, and 89 (29%) were women. While 29% of constituency candidates were women, 43% of Members elected to constituencies in the 2021 election were women. On the regional lists, 223 (68%) candidates were men, and 104 (32%) were women. While 32% of regional list candidates were women, 45% of Members elected via the regional list in the 2021 election were women. Some candidates stood on a regional list as well as for a constituency and have only been counted once in the total figure.*"

These statistics support one of my arguments. We have to be players in any game, in order to stand a chance of winning. We therefore need to look at empowering, equipping and supporting minorities on the pathways to holding positions at a community, local government, and constituency level. In most aspects of life, it is a numbers game. So we have to increase the odds by increasing the numbers of contenders.

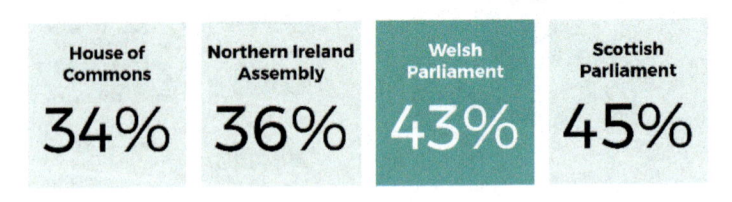

House of Commons	Northern Ireland Assembly	Welsh Parliament	Scottish Parliament
34%	36%	43%	45%

The UK Representation landscape- Gender

LGBTQ and the Welsh Assembly

In 2016 the Independent reported on the Welsh Assembly voting in its first openly gay Assembly Member.[29] As it happens, it was also a female member. Another example of intersectionality.

"Labour candidate and former LGBT Labour co-chair, Hannah Blythyn, has won the Delyn constituency. She won the seat with 9,480 votes, giving her a majority of 3,582," the report declared…as if it were announcing the first moon landing. I look forward to a day when these matters are no longer considered news. But we can only dream.

Jeremy Miles who is also gay, won the Neath seat in the same year. By all accounts, there are three known gay Assembly members in Wales, according to BBC News.[30]

It should also, be noted that the Welsh National Assembly was recognised in 2018[31] as the leading employer for lesbian, gay, bisexual, and transgender people in the latest Stonewall [32] Workplace Equality Index.

---

[29] https://www.independent.co.uk/news/uk/politics/hannah-blythyn-first-ever-openly-gay-politician-elected-to-welsh-assembly-a7015976.html
[30] https://www.bbc.co.uk/news/uk-wales-politics-36230898
[31] https://senedd.wales/senedd-now/news/national-assembly-recognised-as-the-uk-s-top-employer-for-lesbian-gay-bisexual-and-transgender-people/
[32] https://www.stonewall.org.uk/

Hannah Blythyn

Disability and Representation

For a democracy to be truly representative, it needs to reflect the diversity of its citizens. By addressing the barriers faced by disabled individuals in politics, we not only uphold the core principles of democracy, but we also enrich the political landscape with diverse perspectives and experiences. Everyone benefits from a more inclusive and representative political system.

Wales, as part of the UK, has made strides in terms of advocating for the rights of disabled people in various spheres. The political landscape in Wales, shaped by its devolved government, the Welsh Parliament (Senedd Cymru), and other local authorities, is unique in its own right. Yet, the representation of disabled individuals remains an area that requires further attention.

Physical Accessibility in the Welsh Political Arena

Though there have been improvements in accessibility in public buildings across Wales, some older town halls and political venues may still pose challenges for individuals with mobility issues. The architectural heritage of many Welsh towns means there are historic buildings which are challenging to adapt. I do not pretend to not understand the costs involved in making these historical buildings accessible. However, I am very passionate about the fact that we cannot afford to ignore this need. By making these venues inconvenient, if not totally inaccessible, we as a nation are robbing ourselves of the value these potential disabled candidates are able to bring to the Welsh political landscape.

Welsh Language and Communication

The Welsh language, being one of the two official languages of Wales, plays an essential role in its political landscape. Disabled individuals who might already face communication barriers in English may face compounded challenges if Welsh is not their first language, and they require accessible materials in it. I am pleased to report that there are several mechanisms in place to support disabled candidates who are English speakers in the realm of Welsh politics.

Modern assistive technologies, which can aid disabled individuals in accessing digital content, often have multilingual capacities. This means English-speaking disabled candidates can access Welsh content more easily using technologies like screen readers or voice recognition software.

The Senedd has made strides in ensuring its proceedings are accessible. Besides physical accommodations, they provide live translation services, and their website offers both English and Welsh versions, designed to be accessible to users with disabilities.

While support exists, it's important to note that the landscape is ever evolving. Continuous efforts are needed to ensure that English-speaking disabled candidates in Welsh politics receive the necessary support to participate effectively, especially as the push for greater use of the Welsh language in public life continues. It's also crucial for political parties, advocacy groups, and the government to stay updated on the needs of disabled individuals to ensure that the support provided remains relevant and effective.

Stigma and Stereotyping

Attitudes and perceptions about disabled people are not just global or national issues—they are also local. Even within Welsh communities, there can be biases and misconceptions about the capabilities of disabled individuals, which can be a deterrent for potential candidates.

Major parties like Labour, Plaid Cymru, and the Conservatives have diversity agendas, but the extent to which they specifically cater to the needs of disabled individuals varies. It is essential for these parties to recognise and support potential disabled leaders actively.

Recommendations for the Welsh Context

Each of us need to play our small part. Together we can. It is not just an organisation's or one Leader's responsibility. Like I always say, "We go together or not at all!" Here are just a few ideas that should help.

Welsh Government Initiatives: The Welsh Government could spearhead initiatives aimed at promoting disabled representation, providing grants or funds for disabled candidates, and making political education more accessible. I know some effort has been made in this respect but we have a far way to go

Community Engagement: Interest groups platforming disabled hopefuls and providing opportunities to showcase the talent of the disabled hopefuls and not their setbacks. It would also be helpful to engage with local communities and disabled advocacy groups to understand the specific challenges faced within the Welsh context and tailor solutions accordingly.

Promotion of Success Stories: Highlighting success stories of disabled individuals in Welsh politics can serve as inspiration and a counter-narrative to existing biases. This would potentially allow those who actually qualify as disabled, to go public and positively change the narrative about disabilities.

Disability Change Makers in Wales:

1. **Rhian Davies:** Chief Executive of Disability Wales, she has been instrumental in championing the rights of disabled people in Wales. Through her leadership, the organization has influenced policy decisions and raised awareness on key disability issues in Wales.

2. **Tanni Grey-Thompson:** While her impact extends beyond just Wales, as a Welsh former wheelchair racer and now a parliamentarian in the House of Lords, Tanni is an inspirational figure. Her athletic achievements combined with her advocacy for disabled individuals in politics and other spheres make her a significant changemaker.

Both Pippa Britton OBE and Daniel Biddle, have had a significant impact in their respective areas and have become influential figures in the context of disability and resilience in the UK, particularly Wales.

Pippa Britton OBE:

1. **Background:** Pippa Britton is a former Welsh archer who has competed at the highest levels, despite facing physical challenges due to a medical condition.

2. **Advocacy:** Beyond her achievements in sports, Britton has been an advocate for disabled individuals, particularly in the realm of sports. She's been actively involved in several initiatives and organizations that promote sports for people with disabilities.

3. **Roles:** Pippa has also taken on leadership roles in sports administration. For instance, she is Vice Chair for Disability Sport Wales and Vice Chair for the Paralympic Association and has been a vocal advocate for increasing opportunities for disabled athletes.

Daniel Biddle - 7/7 Survivor:

1. **7/7 London Bombings:** Daniel Biddle is a survivor of the 7/7 London bombings in 2005. He was severely injured in the Edgware Road blast, losing both legs, an eye, and suffering a range of other injuries.

2. **Recovery and Resilience:** Following the attack, Biddle faced immense challenges, both physically and mentally. His journey of recovery, resilience, and readjustment has

been inspirational for many. He had to relearn basic functions, and his path was marked by multiple surgeries and rehabilitation sessions.

3. **Advocacy:** After his recovery, Biddle became a motivational speaker and advocate for survivors of terrorist attacks and people with disabilities. His firsthand experiences, combined with his determination to move forward, make his story poignant and influential.

4. **Mental Health:** Daniel Biddle has also spoken about the mental health challenges he faced post the bombings, including PTSD, and has highlighted the importance of psychological support for survivors of such traumatic incidents.

These are just a few examples. Throughout Wales, many other local advocates, community leaders, and organizations tirelessly work to support disabled individuals, advocate for their rights, and ensure they have the resources and platforms they need. The continued efforts of these changemakers, combined with systemic initiatives, will undoubtedly pave the way for a more inclusive and representative political landscape.

HIDING IN PLAIN SIGHT - The Hidden Diversity

9 HIDING IN PLAIN SIGHT - The Hidden Diversity

So, what do I want to interject at this stage? It is important to understand that despite the fact that there are many characteristics… protected characteristics rightly so, of diversity equity and inclusion, it is not straightforward. There are those of us who appear to be privileged, who are suffering from hidden disabilities. In fact, there is this admission that there are unseen disabilities. And I must assert here, that there are unseen diversity issues. There are unseen points of exclusion. There are unseen deficiencies.

There are ways in which people have been othered and they are unable to articulate it because it is not overt, and nobody has taken the time to ask them how they are really coping. So, for example I have seen, and I have met white, blonde beautiful young ladies who have opened up and told me about growing up neurodiverse. They grew up being told they were not up to the mark. They grew up with teachers who did not have the time of day for them. They grew up being laughed at. They grew up being unable to spell. They grew up unable to learn in the way their counterparts learned and so they were left behind, because nobody realised, and nobody acknowledged neurodiversity.

Shazia Hussain

But I will go further on and come into 2023. I have had the privilege of meeting Shazia Hussain who is one of the 2023 Apprentice Stars. Shazia Hussain was diagnosed late in life to be neurodiverse. She got to a remarkably high place within the competition. "Neurodiversity is my superpower, says Shazia. "NOT a hindrance. It allows me to think differently and create original & refreshing ideas that are outside the norm. Even though I struggled to read and write, my neurodiversity wasn't picked up when I was at school. I managed to triumph in spite of the educators not understanding it. I was punished throughout my education because of it. However, if educators and the workplace recognise it and understand it."

To underscore my point about hidden, disabilities and exclusions, no one had any idea they were watching a young lady who was neurodiverse excelling and using the same methods to complete the same task with teammates who had no neurological challenges.

In the workplace, there are so many examples of the neglect to contemplate, neglect to prepare for, and the neglect to provide for those who join our teams, join our workplaces, and our missions. We fail to put policies in place which we actually adhere to and not just file away. We fail to hold our leaders to account to make it their duty to ascertain the full makeup of their teams.

It is my firm belief that we need to prioritise diagnosis of people who are clearly struggling from an early age. Furthermore, when we do have people coming into our teams, like I said earlier in this book, we actually do assessments and skills audits that interrogate personality types and ways of thinking as well. By that means, we get a full understanding of what each member in a team presents with, and what great talents they have, that if we treat with them appropriately, we will benefit.

NEURODIVERSITY IN EDUCATION AND LIFE

The experience of Shazia Hussain provides a vital example of the challenges neurodiverse individuals often encounter in education, employment, and life. Despite her late diagnosis and the struggles, she faced within the competition, she was able to excel, based on her obvious talents and capabilities. However, let us not ignore her story as it also underscores the lack of accommodations and understanding often experienced by neurodiverse school children. Unfortunately, it more often than not, hampers their progress and success.

Neurodiversity is a concept where neurological differences are recognised and respected as any other human variation. These differences can include those diagnosed with dyspraxia, dyslexia, attention deficit hyperactivity disorder, dyscalculia, autistic spectrum, Tourette Syndrome, and others. An understanding of neurodiversity emphasises that these are not deficits, but rather differences that should be respected and accommodated. Nonetheless, too often this is not the case and the neuro diverse are made to feel inconvenient and diminished.

In the Welsh context, the Additional Learning Needs and Education Tribunal (Wales) Act 2018 is a step towards recognising and accommodating diverse learning needs. This act seeks to create a unified system for supporting learners with additional learning needs, including those who are neurodiverse.

However, passing legislation is one thing, and applying legislation it is another matter. If the legislation has no "teeth", it is of no use. So, what gives teeth to legislation? The key to the efficacy of any legislation, is enforcement. There has to be a clear provision for monitoring and enforcement. Those tasked with adherence must also be equipped to monitor and regulate effectively and timely. It's crucial that educators, from primary schools to higher education institutions, are equipped to identify and support diverse learning capabilities. This includes training to recognise neurodiverse students, implementing inclusive teaching strategies, and providing accommodations that level the playing field for these students.

I am pleased to share that in order to ensure enforcement and monitoring of the provisions of the Act, the following mechanisms have been outlined:

1. **Individual Development Plans (IDPs)**: These are statutory documents outlining the learner's ALN and the provision required to meet those needs. The responsibility for maintaining the IDP and ensuring that the provision outlined within it is provided, lies with the school, local authority, or further education institution.

2. **Statutory Roles**: The Act introduces statutory roles of Additional Learning Needs Coordinators (ALNCos) and Designated Lead Officers (DLOs) in schools and local authorities, respectively. ALNCos have the duty to coordinate the school's ALN provision, including the development and review of IDPs. DLOs are responsible for coordinating local authorities' functions under the Act.

3. **Dispute Resolution and Appeal**: If a disagreement arises between a parent or young person and a school or local authority about ALN identification or provision, the Act outlines dispute resolution procedures. These include disagreement resolution services and, ultimately, the right to appeal to the Special Educational Needs

Tribunal for Wales (SENTW). SENTW is an independent body that hears and decides on appeals against decisions made by local authorities on ALN matters.

4. **Inspection and Regulation**: The work of schools and local authorities in implementing the Act will be subject to inspection and regulation by Estyn (the education and training inspectorate for Wales) and the Care Inspectorate Wales. They can evaluate how well schools and local authorities meet their duties under the Act. Their reports provide essential oversight and can trigger improvements where necessary.

5. **Duty to provide Information**: There is a statutory duty for schools, local authorities, and health bodies to share information relating to ALNs and provision. This helps to ensure transparency and accountability in how ALN services are provided.

6. **Implementation and Monitoring by the Welsh Government**: The Welsh Government will oversee the implementation of the Act and monitor progress. It also has powers to issue statutory guidance (for instance, the ALN Code) that schools and local authorities must have regard to.

While the Additional Learning Needs and Education Tribunal (Wales) Act 2018 provides for robust enforcement and monitoring mechanisms, it is crucial that these are fully implemented and resourced. This will ensure that every child or young person with ALN can have their needs met effectively, enabling them to reach their full educational potential.

According to the Annual Population Survey, as of 2021, 3.7% of people in Wales reported that they had a learning difficulty (note that this does not solely refer to neurodiversity). This percentage, however minor it might seem, represents a considerable number of individuals who might require different approaches to learning.

The importance of the above cannot be overstated. Ensuring that neurodiverse students receive the support they need has numerous benefits. At the risk of being repetitive, I must underscore that this approach, fosters an inclusive learning environment that respects and values diversity. It ensures all students, regardless of their neurological makeup, have the opportunity to reach their potential. It also contributes to overall societal inclusivity, as students who receive appropriate support are more likely to succeed in their future careers, such as Shazia Hussain.

Shazia's experience in The Apprentice serves as a reminder that neurodiversity is often 'invisible' (hiding in plain sight) and that without appropriate accommodations, neurodiverse individuals can be at a disadvantage. As Shazia herself argues, being treated the same as everyone else does not necessarily equate to fairness or equality. In a society that values equality of opportunity, it's essential that we move towards understanding and supporting neurodiversity in all aspects of life, including in our educational institutions.

It is irrefutable that recognising and accommodating diverse learning capabilities, including neurodiversity, is a crucial aspect of education, not just in Wales but everywhere. It's about ensuring that all students, regardless of their neurological differences, are given an equal opportunity to succeed. As educators and policymakers, the goal should be to create an inclusive and supportive learning environment that celebrates diversity and allows all learners to flourish[33].

In my research, I looked into disability within the Welsh Assembly, and it is interesting to see one of the statements within a report[34]

"Even if a more restrictive notion of disability was used, only including major impairments, we should expect to see 65 disabled MPs. Yet, after the General Election in 2015 there were only 3 MPs who declared or were publicly identified as being disabled, which increased to 5 after the 2017 General Election.28 Jul 2021

There are disabled amongst us who are hiding in plain sight because they are afraid and ashamed. Afraid of not being given a fair chance and ashamed that although they can pass, they are not fully fitted within what the rest of us ignorant thinkers, call normal. Therein lies the real shame and the absolute pity.

---

[33]

1. Annual Population Survey, 2021
2. Additional Learning Needs and Education Tribunal (Wales) Act 2018

[34] https://www.gov.uk/government/publications/barriers-to-elected-office-for-disabled-people/barriers-to-elected-office-for-disabled-people

And there are the overtly disabled who still not getting sufficient provision there are still venues, where the disabled are entering through the kitchens to access fancy events. Sometimes, they are supposed to be recipients of Awards at the very event! Shame on us!

What about those of us who we would like to hide away from our sights and our contemplation, for fear and for shame? I am referring to those of us who have alternative sexual orientation. Who are we to judge? Who are we to decide who deserves our love. Who are we to decide who deserves our priority?

It takes me to an incredibly sad story I was told about what happened to one of my classmates. I will not name him out of respect for his family and to not cause any undue pain and suffering. But this dear friend of mine that I went to school with…he was a joy to be in class with. He was funny. He was caring. He was kind. But eventually we found out after the fact that he was gay. This dear friend of ours moved to another country and I was told recently, when I got back in touch with some of my classmates, that unfortunately he passed away.

That was shocking enough. But it further shattered my heart to hear that when his body was flown back to his home country, to be buried where he was born, and where his family lives…his body was met with riots the roads were blocked. They would not have him buried there. My heart bleeds for that. Who are we to decide that a mother's son cannot come home to rest because they did not live the way we believe? Who set us up as the moral arbiters, judge, jury, and condemners of people?

We have got to learn to disagree and love and respect and honour. Without doing that, we would have lost our humanity and there will not be a world worth fighting for.

MASTERING DIVERSITY

10 MASTERING DIVERSITY

In this closing chapter I would like to share with you my thoughts, my beliefs and my convictions as to what it really means to ***master diversity***. I would like to give my personal takeaway from all the very many important concepts, facts, legislation, research and advocacy around diversity and inclusion which I have documented and commented on for our consideration. If my invitation to master diversity is accepted, how would I like you to treat with it? My suggestion is mastery over anything is a skill that is transferable. I will therefore simplify mastery and mastery of diversity in this short chapter. I am always of the view that we like to complicate things too much. Complications, exclude and that would be a contradiction in terms, should I allow that in this book about inclusion. So, what does it take to master anything…to gain full mastery over any skill, hobby talent or pursuit?

MAKE IT YOUR FOCUS!

It is all about making something the focus of your time, of your meditation, of your research, of your contemplations and of your interrogations. You cannot truly master something by flicking in and out. And you certainly cannot master it by "skim reading" the signs, as we journey through life.

How do we make Diversity a focus?

If this new passion is a hobby, we move heaven and earth to get our friends to join in with us. While we are at work, we are planning on what we are going to do afterwards. We are always thinking how we are going to engage more with this person or this pursuit? Do you see where I'm going with this?

Nevertheless, we need to first of all be sure about what it is that we are trying to get people to come on board with. We need to understand the values for ourselves. We need to be convinced about all the areas of it that affect our lives and those within our world. Once we come to grips with DEI and we focus on it and make it our point of duty to consistently keep abreast with what is happening, we begin the journey to mastery.

AWARENESS IS KEY

Awareness of the fact that we do not have all the answers is paramount. When we are aware that we do not have all the answers then we seek for information to help us to get all the facts. We have to start taking stock of our communities, our regions and our "worlds". We need to become aware of who are, which sector and intersections we represent in the diversity conundrum. In my case I am a Black Caribbean woman of a certain age and with a certain status, with a particular way of thinking and a unique way of being with certain predispositions. But I am aware because of the work that I do that it is important to consider other people. I need to then master my focus around aspects of diversity equity and inclusion that are in my world that I can be a part of the change in, and I can have influence over others to participate in. I therefore make diversity and inclusion my focus. I am also learning more about aspects of it that I am aware are more applicable to my context. By so doing I can respond accurately and knowledgeably to those who seek my help and I thereby make my difference in the ways that it matters

Awareness of our environment is also key. I'm reminded of this Jingle in *Sesame Street*. Some of you are too old to remember and I'm not sure if it was played in the United Kingdom. But where I grew up there was Sesame Street for children and there was a song asking "who are the people in your neighbourhood the…the postal worker the grocer, and teacher… and that we need to know who the people in our neighbourhood are. So, I put it to you *are you aware of the people in your neighbourhood*? Who are the people in your neighbourhood and why does that matter? Who are the refugees? Who are the disabled? Who are the mentally challenged? Who are the ones from a lower socio-economic background? Who are the ones who are struggling with their sense of self? Who are the ones who were adopted and went through the foster care system and as a result of that they have difficulty with attachment? Who are the ones who are neurodiverse and cognitively diverse who seem to be problematic, but it's just that it is symptomatic of something completely different which we should take the time to learn about? Who are the people that wear those colourful garbs, who have jewels on their teeth and the most amazing colours in their hair? Who are the people in our neighbourhood and what do they need from us?

SHARE

And then it takes me to sharing. In order to master anything, you must understand how to not just use it but also how to share it. How to make it available to others. How to make it safe. Now, what do I mean by that? How do I share it? It is pretty much harking back to couple chapters on representation when I gave the example of how some people become really angry when they feel they're not represented.

When we pursue mastering diversity, we do not want to be condescending. We do not want to be judgmental and do not want to be confrontational. There is no room for accusations. We want to be all embracing we want to be tolerant. We must be patient. An understanding of a life lived mastering diversity makes us committed to being kind. We are moved to share our good news that things can be better whilst being tolerant of those who take a little bit longer to understand. Our goal is to influence others and self-replicate. Sometimes those who take a little bit longer to understand, once they finally do, they become the greatest supporters, work the hardest and campaign vigorously for the benefit of others.

Let me end with this analogy. When we fall in love and we believe we've found something that's of great value, what do we do? The first thing that we do is tell our friends about it. If it is an individual, we bombard our friends with how amazing this person is. We want them to buy into this person and this idea of this new relationship, this newfound love, this newfound friend that you have. This is what I would like us all to do by the end of this book…fall in love with DEI and share it gushingly with all who will listen.

TAKE YOUR TIME

It takes time…you're *mastering* diversity. It Is going to take time. In this book I have harked back to historical times in Wales, back to the time when coal was king, historical times in politics in Wales and historical times in my own life in the Caribbean. I spoke of historical times in United Kingdom and so it is important for us to grasp that disparities developed over time and things **will** get better over time. We are setting the stage and we are a part of a race which started a long time ago. In this book I've quoted several experts, several advocates, several organisations and several politicians who have heretofore carried the flame, ran with the baton and now it's our turn. Now it is **our** time. But you have to understand it will take time. It will take time to listen to other's opinions. Time to platform other voices. Time to host events. Time for fireside chats. Time to lobby and time to petition. Time, like I have taken to write this book. One thing is sure, we will never achieve anything if we are not prepared to give it the time.

Finally, we are only responsible for what we did in our time and with the time we had available to make change. Let us not get caught navel gazing and second guessing our abilities or regretting missed opportunities. We need to be aware of the fact that we are in a chain, and we are links. Our job is to remain a strong link. The great "Chain Maker", The Lord of all, will craft the final product. Our only concern is not to be the odd weak link.

Evolution is par for the course

Things are ever changing. They're ever growing and ever developing. It is important to remember that in our pursuing we are prepared for evolution. As we are learning, the very thing that we are interrogating is evolving. It is dynamic. There is an old saying that one should never take a photograph of one's life. Your life is not a picture. Diversity is an amazing moving target. What was acceptable in the past will get you "cancelled" or incarcerated now. There was a time when saying "coloured" was OK. Now people resent being called "coloured". I for one would prefer you to call me black. There were times when it was OK to make jokes about Black people, Irish people and others, on a regular basis. Now those things are no longer allowed. "There's a brown girl in the ring" is a song I still love. But it's not allowed. There was a time when Tom Jones' song *Delilah* caused absolutely no offence. So, as you can see it seems like a contradiction in terms but when you are mastering, when you're making it your focus, when you're being aware of the many nuances of it, even if you trip over some things, you will finish your course.

Resolve

Mastery of anything requires unflinching resolve. In mastering diversity, I would ask you to resolve to never stop. Resolve to never give up your focus on mastering diversity. Resolve to be a part of the change. Resolve not be the negative influence that perpetuates instead of mitigates. Resolve to use love and not hate. Resolve to be tolerant and considerate and not dismissive. Resolve to practise allyship in its truest form. Resolve to educate yourself about what really matters. Resolve to be the best version of yourself and to use all your best efforts to master diversity equality equity AND inclusion

Make it your focus!
Awareness is key
Share
Take your time
Evolution is par for the course
Resolve

CONCLUSION

There are so many more stories I could tell, research findings, I could cite and arguments I could postulate. But this book is not about completeness. It is an invitation to treat. It is a cry from a collective heart and passion for change within our world and more particularly, the Welsh region. Let us join hands and hearts. Let us create more opportunities for conversations around diversity. Let us give voice to the voiceless, representation to the underrepresented, unearth hidden exclusions, make reparations, and build engagement. Alone, I can do nothing but together we can… ***WE GO TOGETHER…OR NOT AT ALL!***

ABOUT THE AUTHOR

Multiple Award-winning Bestselling Author, TEDX Speaker, Business Strategist and Diversity and Inclusion Thought Leader, Bernie Davies, is a business strategist and Visibility Specialist. Davies is a Business Wales and Equal Power Equal Voice Mentor, The Ambassador for the Commonwealth Entrepreneur Club, sits on the Boards of the Public Services Ombudsman for Wales, Women's Business Club, Fio Arts Charity and has been awarded Ethnic Minority Welsh Women's Award 2023, Lifetime Achievement Award, Ambassador for Peace Award 2022 by the prestigious Universal Peace Federation, Women's Business Club Diversity and Inclusion and Outstanding Speaker Awards 2021 and 2022 respectively, Swansea Black Icon 2018, Top 100 Woman in Business in Wales 2017, Excellence in Business Award 2017 for Black History Month and was featured on ITV Wales's Face To Face series for her life and work on April 13th, 2023.

Bernie has been privileged to share her thought leadership at the United Nations, The House of Lords, London Excel Arena, the Royal Society London, global and national institutions of higher learning; her famous mantra being, "We go together, or not at all."

NOTES

NOTES

NOTES

NOTES

NOTES

NOTES

Printed in Great Britain
by Amazon